Clas,-- Haiku

An Anthology of
Poems by

Bashō

and his Followers

Translated and Annotated by
Asatarō Miyamori

DOVER PUBLICATIONS, INC.
Mineola, New York

Copyright

Published in the United Kingdom by David & Charles, Brunel House, Forde Close, Newton Abbot, Devon TQ12 4PU.

Bibliographical Note

This Dover edition, first published in 2002, contains material selected from *An Anthology of Haiku Ancient and Modern*, translated and annotated by Asatarō Miyamori, originally published by Maruzen Company Ltd., Tokyo, in 1932.

Library of Congress Cataloging-in-Publication Data

Classic haiku : an anthology of poems by Basho and his followers / translated and annotated by Asatarō Miyamori.

p. cm.

Both in English and Japanese (romanized form only).

"... selected from An anthology of haiku, ancient and modern ... originally published by Maruzen ... in 1932."—Copyright page.

ISBN 0-486-42221-6 (pbk.)

1. Haiku—Translation into English. I. Matsuo, Basho, 1644–1694. II. Miyamori, Asataro, 1869–1952. III. Anthology of haiku, ancient and modern.

PL782.E3 C525 2002
895.1'04108—dc21

2002073634

Manufactured in the United States of America
Dover Publications, Inc., 31 East 2nd Street, Mineola, N.Y. 11501

CONTENTS

Introduction :

INTRODUCTION

I

Haiku* (俳句) and Epigrams

The *haiku* (俳句) is the shortest of Japanese poems, consisting of three lines of five, seven and five syllables respectively, i.e. of seventeen syllables all told, and in it seven or eight, at most ten words are counted. Here are examples:—

Tsurigane ni
Tomarite nemuru
Kochō kana

Upon the temple bell
A butterfly is sleeping well. By Buson

Ara-umi ya
Sado ni yokotō
Ama-no-gawa

The sea is wild! The Milky Way extends
Far over to the island of Sado. By Bashō

The *haiku* is written in a kind of verse; but, unlike the *tanka,* which is the next shortest poem of thirty-one syllables, and all other types of Japanese songs and poems, it is a peculiar form of wit, concentrated to the last degree, too short and rather too stiff to sing. It is subject to the traditional limit

* *Haiku* is pronounced somewhat like "hike," not "hake."

of three lines and seventeen syllables; but, as is the case with all other types of Japanese poetry, it has no metre and no rhyme. It is true that almost all Japanese words, like Italian words, end in vowels so that they sound rather smooth and musical. But most of the words employed in poetry, except in some modern poems, are pure Japanese words in which the vowels sound short. Therefore rhyming would be of no value. For instance, in the following verse by Bashō:—

Yagate shinu
Keshiki wa miezu
Semi no koe

There is no sign in the cicadas' cry
That they are just about to die.

Shinu of the first line accidentally rhymes with *miezu* of the second line; but the vowels sound short and consequently have no effect, compared with "cry" and "die" in the translation. It is true that many Japanese words of Chinese origin called *kango* are sometimes used in *haiku* for the sake of vigour of sound, which pure Japanese words lack, but they are never employed for rhyming purposes. Again, there is no stress or force accent* in the Japanese language, which naturally prevents the existence of metres in Japanese poetry. In a word, the absence of metres and of rhyme is what distinguishes Japanese from European verse.

In the Japanese language, unlike the European languages, pronouns are very rarely used, there are no articles and in

* It must be borne in mind that the Japanese language has pitch or musical accent.

haiku, very few grammatical changes of verbs. Therefore, in *haiku* which consist of very few words, the content is comparatively rich. For instance, the following verse by Issa does not contain "it," "they" and "their."

Mino ueno
Kane tomo shirade
Yūsuzumi

Unaware 'tis their life's sunset bell,
They enjoy the cool of evening.

Bashō's famouse verse:—

Furuike ya
Kawazu tobikomu
Mizu no oto

The ancient pond!
A frog plunged—splash!

does not contain "The" and "A"; therefore even to a Japanese, if he has no knowledge as to the circumstances in which Bashō composed this verse, it is not clear whether it is "an old pond" or "the old pond" and whether "some frogs" or "a frog" is meant. Again *tobikomu* may mean "plunged" or "plunges." Compared with painting, the Japanese language is like a sketch in Indian ink, while the European languages, which are more exact in the manner of expression, are like a detailed painting in water colours or in oil. It is, therefore, hardly necessary to say that the translations in the present volume, though they are so simple and short, ought to be clearer to European readers than the original verses are to Japanese readers.

Haiku make use not only of elegant, classical words of purely Japanese origin but also of some words of Chinese origin, and of colloquial and rarely even vulgar words and a few words of European origin. But inasmuch as, from their essential nature, *haiku* require the maximum economy of words, not a loose colloquial, but a compact, literary style is employed. Moreover, this strict economy has necessitated the employment of several particles called *kireji* or "cutting words"—words which terminate a sentence or a phrase. Of these "cutting words," *ya* and *kana* are of the greatest importance. It is no exaggeration to say that they are the only "cutting words" worthy of discussion. Opinion differs as to their significance, but I think it is safe to say that they imply an exclamation of slight degree.

Nanohana ya
Tsuki wa higashi ni
Hi wa nishi ni

What an expanse of rape-flowers,
With the moon east and the sun west! **By Buson**

Fuji hitotsu
Uzumi nokoshite
Wakaba kana

How luxuriant the young foliage,
Leaving only Mount Fuji unburied! **By Buson**

But it is my opinion that it is often better to ignore the exclamatory sense of *kana* and *ya* in translations.

Tsurigane ni
Tomarite nemuru
Kochō kana

Upon the temple bell
A butterfly is sleeping well.

It would be awkward, in order to reproduce the exclamatory sense of *kana*, to add " Behold ! " before " Upon the temple bell " or " Ah ! " before " A butterfly is sleeping well."

Ya and *kana* are the most developed, the most refined, the most solemn of all " cutting words."

Comparing it with painting, the *haiku* is like a sketch or the outlines of a sketch. To stretch the comparison further, the *haiku* is but the title of a picture, nay a suggestion for one. It is hardly necessary to say that even in a sketch of " a butterfly sleeping on the temple bell," outlines of the belfry as well as the bell and the butterfly ought to be represented, while in the *haiku* only the focus of a momentary impression of the scene is hinted at. Generally speaking, in the *haiku* an objective description is given, often omitting the verb, and the poet's subjective sentiment is left to the reader's imagination. Pregnancy and suggestiveness, brevity and ellipsis are the soul and life of a *haiku*. If the poet gives full expression to his feelings in this extremely small verse, there remains very little space for description, so that the resultant poem may be applied to any other similar cases. To write a good *haiku*, it is absolutely necessary to describe the particular features of a given theme as fully as possible. In doing so there is little space for expressing the poet's feelings. A *haijin* or *kaiku* poet of eminent merit leaves a great deal to the association of ideas and imagination of the reader. He does not himself wonder or admire but makes the reader do so.

Kare-eda ni
Karasu no tomarikeri
Aki no kure

A crow is perched on a bare branch;
It is an autumn eve. By Bashō

Such a *haiku* as this is generally considered an ideal realistic or objective verse. It describes only what the poet observes and seems to signify nothing else; but it may well be considered a poem symbolizing a dreary autumn evening. The poet does not spend a single word upon the loneliness of autumn twilight, but the reader is profoundly impressed by the apparently artless description.

Waga yuki to
Omoeba karushi
Kasa no ue

The snow upon my hat
Feels light, being mine own. By Kikaku

This verse is but a bare expression of the poet's subjective sentiment, and by no means a supremely good poem, although it is a famous one. An ideal *haiku* is one in which a natural event is described as it is, and the poet's emotion does not appear on the surface. Compare the following two verses:—

Mitsukushita
Me wa shiragiku ni
Modori keri

My eyes which had seen all came back,
Back to the white chrysanthemums. By Isshō

Kigiku shiragiku
Sonohoka no na wa
Nakumo gana

Yellow and white chrysanthemums;
Would that there were no other names! By Ransetsu

The latter verse is too plainspoken, too subjective, in the eulogy of the yellow and the white chrysanthemums; while the former is an objective description which is more suggestive and more impressive.

As has been seen above, every *haiku* contains a word referring to one or other of the four seasons. Eor instance, in:—

Upon the temple bell
A butterfly is sleeping well.

"butterfly" is a noun referring to spring. It is true there are butterflies also in the other seasons; but when the *haijin* says simply "a butterfly," he means "a spring butterfly," while "butterflies" in the other seasons are modified by the name of the particular season, as "a butterfly of summer or of autumn." This is one of the conventions in *haiku*.

Ara-umi ya
Sado ni yokotō
Ama-no-gawa

The sea is wild! The Milky Way extends
Far over to the island of Sado. By Bashō

"The Milky Way" is a noun belonging to early autumn because the Milky Way is most clearly visible in this season.

Kumo wo fumi
Kasumi wo suuya
Agehibari

How the skylark soars,
Treading on the cloud,
Inhaling the haze! By Shiki

It is hardly necessary to say "skylark" belongs to spring. The cicada and the frog are conventionally considered to belong respectively to summer and spring. Inasmuch as each *haiku* contains generally one "season-word," the *haiku* may well be called a literature of the seasons. The *tanka* also attaches importance to the seasons, so that we have sections for the four seasons in any anthology of *tanka*. But it contains also several other sections, such as "Love," "Journeys" and "The Uncertainty of Life," in which referrence to the seasons is not necessary.

Here is an example:—

Shinoburedo
Iro ni deni keri
Waga koi wa
Mono ya omōto
Hito no tō made

Although I strive hard to conceal
The passion which my bosom tasks,
My visage shows the pain I feel,
Till men ask what torments my heart.
By Taira no Kanemori

Again, in *tanka* "Love" is an important subject, while it is very rarely employed as a theme in *haiku*. And all *haiku* dealing with "Love," "Journey" and such other human affairs contain season-words.

Here are examples:—

Koi to yū
Kusemono satte
Yuki samushi

That rogue called Love having left me,
How cold snow feels to me! By Jakushi

Koibito wo Omō

Okite mitsu
Nete mitsu kaya no
Hirosa kana

Longing for My Sweetheart

I sit up or lie down and yet,
How large is the mosquito-net!
By Ukihashi (a poetess)

Shitei no Musubi Sema Hoshiku Iwareshi Hito ni

Hana no nai
Ki ni yoru hito zo
Tada narane

To a Man who Asks me To be his Teacher

Ah! he is not a common man
Who turns to a flowerless tree. By Onitsura

Haijin Isshō no Shi wo Itamu

Tsuka mo ugoke
Waga naku koe wa
Aki no kaze

In Sorrow for the Death of the Haijin Isshō

Oh, grave-mound, move!
My wailing is the autumn wind. By Bashō

"Seventeen syllables" and "reference to the seasons" are the two essential elements in *haiku.* As to why the seasons are such an important factor in *haiku,* two or three reasons may be given. The first reason is traditional, in that the first hemistich of linked poems which later developed into the *haiku,* as will be seen in the next chapter, always contained a season-word as the essential element. Next, the insertion of a season-word makes the tiny verse highly suggestive. A vivid idea of the season of the particular case gives the reader a clearer impression of the theme treated of than otherwise. The third reason is this. The Japanese are passionate lovers of Nature. Every feature, every phase, every change of Nature in the four seasons powerfully excites their delicate æsthetic sense. Not to speak of cherry-blossom viewing picnics which are the custom among all people, high and low, young and old, the Japanese often row out in pleasure-boats on the sea or on a lake to enjoy the harvest moon; they often climb hills for views of the "silver world" of snow; they often visit rivers in darkness to contemplate fireflies; they often climb wooded mountains to delight in the rich brocade of frost-bitten maple leaves; they often listen with ecstasy to the songs of frogs, of which Ki no Tsurayuki, an ancient poet, says:—"the frog* dwelling in the water—all living things sing songs." On autumn evenings singing-insects kept in cages are sold at street-stalls; and townsfolk listen to them in order to hear "the voices of autumn." And naturally enough, men of taste, particularly poets, while enjoying these scenes, compose verses on the spur of the moment. *Haijin* often take a stroll into the country in search of poetic inspiration from the changing features of Nature. They take pen and paper with them and when happy ideas for versification cross their minds, they jot them down and afterwards finish them up into verses. Such strolls are called *ginkō* or "poetic outings."

The following are some of the most important season-words and the commonest themes for *haijin*:—

SPRING (February, March and April):—Springtime, Haze, Snow left unmelted, Spring rain, the Spring moon, the *Uguisu* or Japanese nightingale, which is the sweetest bird of passage, Larks, Swallows, Butterflies, Frogs whose songs (*not* croaking) are appreciated by Japanese poets, Cherry-blossoms which are the most beautiful of Japanese flowers and so highly appreciated that when the *haijin* mentions "the flower," simply, he means the cherry-flower, Plum-blossoms which are considered the next best flowers, Violets, Willows, Camellias, Peach-blossoms, Wistarias, Peonies, Azaleas.

SUMMER (May, June, and July):—Summertime, *Koromogae*, or "Changing clothes" (In Old Japan on the first of April of the lunar calendar, i.e. about May of the solar calendar, spring suits were changed for summer ones), the May rains (In May of the lunar calendar, i.e. June of the solar calendar, it rains for some three weeks in succession), *Yūsuzumi*, or "Enjoying the cool evening breeze," Cuckoos, Fireflies, Cicadas, Goldfish, Dragonflies, Morning-glories, Lotus-flowers, Poppy flowers, Summer chrysanthemums, Lilies.

---

* The frog referred to here, some authorities on Japanese poetry assert, is a peculiar kind of frog called *kajika* which is noted for its particularly sweet voice. Be it so, *haijin* appreciate the cry of even an ordinary frog and they say "frogs sing," not "frogs croak."

AUTUMN (August, September and October):—Autumn evenings, the Milky Way, the Harvest moon (the best full moon of August 15th of the lunar calendar or of September 22 or 23 of the solar calendar; the harvest moon is so highly appreciated that when the *haijin* says simply "the moon," "to-night's moon," or "*meigetsu*,"* or "the bright moon," he means the harvest moon), Wild geese, Crows, Woodpeckers, Quails, Insects (several insects whose sweet notes are highly esteemed), Chrysanthemums, Maple leaves and all other trees whose leaves turn scarlet, Scarecrows, Paulownias, Ivy.

WINTER (November, December and January):—Winter, Falling leaves, Frost, Ice, Hail, Snow, the Winter moon, Withered fields, the Close of the year, New Year's Eve, Camellias, New Year's Day, Mandarin ducks.

Some British and American writers call the *haiku* "the Japanese epigram," on the ground that in length it resembles the shortest European poems—the Greek, the Roman and modern epigrams. But this epithet is quite inappropriate, inasmuch as, on the average, the *haiku* is much shorter than the epigrams, which sometimes run to twenty or thirty lines, and are quite different in content, in subject matter, from the other. The epigrams, for the most part, treat of human affairs and aim chiefly at humour, cynicism and satire. On the other hand, the *haiku* treat principally of Nature—natural beauties and natural phenomena and always make some referrence to the seasons; and humour is considered bad taste in *haiku*.

Kaze ikka
Ninō atsusa ya
Uchiwa-uri

A load of wind upon his back,
How hot he is—the fan-pedlar! By Kakō

---

* *Meigetsu* is often represented by two Chinese characters (名月) signifying "the famous moon," but both "the bright moon" and "the famous moon" mean the harvest moon.

This verse is very witty and humorous, but is not an excellent *haiku*. The following are typical epigrams:—

The Epitaph on Saon

Here lapped in hallowed slumber Saon lies,
Asleep, not dead; a good man never dies.

By Callimachus, a Greek poet

On Acerra

Acerra smells of last night's wine you say,
Don't wrong Acerra; he topes on till day.

By Martial, the most famous Roman epigrammatist

To Velox

You say my epigrams, Velox, too long are;
You nothing write; sure yours are shorter far.

By Martial

About Death

Why shrink from Death, the parent of repose,
The cure of sickness and all human woes?
As through the tribes of men he speeds his way,
Once, and but once, his visit he will pay;
Whilst pale diseases, harbingers of pains
Close on each other crowd—an endless train.

By Agathias

The Balance of Europe

Now Europe's balanced, neither side prevails;
For nothing's left in either of the scales. By Pope

Beat Your Pate

You beat your pate and fancy wit will come,
Knock as you please, there's nobody at home. By Pope

An Epitaph Upon Himself

I strove with none, for none was worth my strife;
    Nature I loved, and next to Nature, Art;
I warmed both hands before the fire of life:
    It sinks; and I am ready to depart. By Landor

The Staff and the Paddle

Thou canst not wave thy staff in air,
    Or dip thy paddle in the lake,
But it carves the bow of beauty there,
    And the ripples in rhyme the oar forsake.
By Emerson

Popularity

Such kings of shreds have wooed and won her,
    Such crafty knaves her laurel owned,
It has become almost an honour
    Not to be crowned. By Aldrich

These epigrams bear a greater resemblance to *senryū* or witty poems of seventeen syllables which were originated by Karai Hachiemon (1718–1790) who had the pen name of Senryū ("The River Willow"). Senryū are more biting and often more vulgar.

The following are typical *senryū*:—

Kurombo ga
Kurombo wo unde
Anshin shi

A negress feels relieved,
Giving birth to a negro. By Saraku

Shibai mita
Ban wa teishu ga
Iya ni nari

The night she sees a play,
A woman hates her husband. By Hammonsen

Itsumademo
Ikite iru ki no
Kawo bakari

Each and every face looks as if
They expect to live for ever. By Shimpei

Ippon no
Matchi ni yami no
Tajirokinu

A single match
Makes darkness flinch. By Mannen

Jinkaku no
Ura wo onna ni
Nozokareru

The secrets of fine character
Are peeped into by women. By Kōsui

Konnen mo
Aikawarazu to
Isha mo kuru

The physician calls with the greeting
"Please give me your patronage this year too."
By Ryūga

Dokubō ni
Shinran wo shiri
Yaso wo shiri

In the solitary cell
I knew Shinran and Christ. By Yushun

Hitotsu hi ni
Shiro to kuro to
Kiina hito

Beneath one sun do live
White, black and yellow men. By Sekifu

Jinsei wa
Saien dekinu
Drama kana

Ah, human life is a drama
Which cannot be produced again. By Moshi

Kanemochi no
Ie no shita nimo
Jishintai

Beneath a millionaire's house lies
Also the earthquake zone. By Ichigen

Meni mienu
Kami nareba koso
Shinjirare

God is believed in,
Because He can't be seen. By Shimpei

Nusumi-gokoro no
Naiga kojiki no
Jiman nari

It is a beggar's pride
That he has not a thieving mind. By Hammonsen

Shinsetsu ni
Oshiete yatte
Suri mo nori

Kindly advising about the route,
The pickpocket too got on the train. By Goyō

Yoku mireba
Teno todoku dake
Shibui kaki

All persimmons within my reach
Have proved to be astringent.

Ano hoshi ga
Futari no kuni to
Shijin meki

The couple say, like poets,
"See! That star is our country." By Isamu

Ko wo utta
Kane inazuma no
Yōni kie

The price of the daughter he sold
Has vanished like lightning.

Kōkō no
Shitai toki ni wa
Oya wa nashi

One's parents are no more
When one wants to do his duty to them.

Itsumade ka
Jūku jūku no
Shirabyōshi

For ever, dancing girls
Are nineteen years of age.

Chōnai de
Shiranu wa teishu
Bakari nari

All the town is aware
Except her own husband.

As we have already seen, brevity and suggestiveness are the soul and life of a *haiku*. It is, therefore, a self-evident truth that the translation of a *haiku*, as far as possible, must be as simple, concise and laconic as the original; and paraphrasing is out of the question. A translation is a translation, not a paraphrase. Of course, it is often, rather too often, necessary, for a foreign reader who has no knowledge of the technique of *haiku*, to give a long paraphrase in addition to the translation. But the translation should be faithful to the original as far as possible. The above cited verse on the butterfly by Buson is translated as follows by Dr. Curtis Page, an American authority on Japanese poetry :—

The butterfly sleeps well
Perched upon the temple bell. . . .
Until it rings!

The last line "Until it rings!" which was never intended by the poet, spoils the entire poem, nay, utterly destroys it. In this form, it is no *haiku* but a clumsy, ill-understood paraphrase. This poem is an objective description of a momentary impression. Suppose the poet sees the scene at about one o'-clock; then according to Dr. Page's translation, the butterfly is imagined to sleep on until the dusk when the temple bell rings.

Nevertheless, it is sometimes necessary, when the original is obscure in meaning, even for Japanese readers, to add in the translation two or three words which are not found in the original. For instance, in the elegy on the death of his beloved child by the ancient poet Raizan :—

Haru no yume
Kino chigawanu ga
Urameshii

A spring dream!
Pity it is that I have not gone mad!

" A spring dream ! " is quite meaningless to most Japanese readers, much more to foreigners. Therefore, I have added four words and translated the poem as follows :—

Life is fleeting as a spring dream.
Pity it is that I have not gone mad !

Let it be mentioned in passing that in Japanese classics fleeting life is often compared to a spring night's dream, as it is in the first paragraph of the *Heike Monogatari* or " The Tale of The Taira Family."

Again some *haiku* end abruptly in the middle of the description. For instance, Issa, the ancient poet, says in his famous verse on the death of his beloved child.

Tsuyu no yo wa
Tsuyu no yo nagara
Sarinagara

Life is the morning dew ;
'Tis true but. . . .

It is hardly necessary to say the sorrow-stricken bard means " but how sad this is ! " and the conjunction *sarinagara* which means " but " is extremely smooth and melodious and the whole poem, though incomplete in construction, sounds exceedingly sweet and musical. So I have translated this poem in two ways :—

Life is the morning dew ;
'Tis true, but well-a-day !

Life is the morning dew, bards say ;
'Tis true, indeed, but well-a-day !

Mr. Basil Hall Chamberlain, who probably did not know the verse is an elegy, translates:—

Granted this dewdrop world is but
A dewdrop world—this granted, yet. . . .

and gives a long explanation to the effect that life is transient but it has joys and permanent elements and is quite enjoyable.

In the present volume I have translated *haiku* in three ways:—the majority of them are written in two lines of Iambic verse, a considerable number in two lines of Trochaic verse, and a few in three lines of free verse. And in the translation of *haiku* of refined style I sometimes use rhyme and the solemn style, and rarely I use rather slangy expressions in poems containing such.

II

A Brief History of Haiku (俳句)

The type of Japanese literature which arose first in order is the *tanka* (短歌) or "short poem" which consists of 5 lines of 5, 7, 5, 7, 7 syllables respectively, i. e. of 31 syllables as follows :—

Shirogane mo (5), *kugane* mo tama mo* (7), *nani senni* (5),
masareru takara, (7) *koni shikame yamo* (7).

Silver, gold and jewels—
They are to me but trash up-piled;
Nothing can compare with
A treasure of a child. By Yamanoue no Okura

This form of poetry has been in vogue for over twenty centuries down to the present day.

The *haiku* (俳句), the shortest form of Japanese poetry, consisting of 3 lines of 5, 7, 5 syllables respectively, i. e. of 17 syllables, came into existence far later than the short poem; but it is much more popular: it is composed, throughout the empire, by people of all stations in life, men and women, young and old. Lafcadio Hearn's remark applies with special significance to the case of *haiku* :—"Poetry in Japan is universal as the air. It is felt by everybody. It is read by everybody. It is composed by almost everybody—irrespective of class and

* *Kugane* (gold) or, popularly, *kogane*. *Kugane* is the pronunciation of the days of the poet who lived twelve centuries ago.

condition." In this sense the Japanese people may well be called a nation of poets and poetesses.

Before speaking of the origin of the *haiku*, it is necessary to devote a few paragraphs to the origin and development of the *renga* (連歌) or "linked poem" which made its appearance next to the short poem. It is of exactly the same form as the short poem; but it was a sort of literary pastime in which the first hemistich of 5, 7, 5 syllables was composed by one man and the second hemistich of 7, 7 syllables by another. In contradistinction to the short poem and the *haiku* which are both serious verses, the linked poem is comic and humorous, in content and language, making free use of pivot-words and associated words, sometimes employing even slang, and often Chinese expressions which are not found in the short poem and sometimes found in the *haiku*.

The linked poem has a long history. Its origin is usually dated far back to a variety of the short poem composed jointly by an aged man and by the heroic Imperial prince Yamato-takeru-no-Mikoto who lived in the 1st century. This literary pastime came into a gradually increasing fashion among courtiers and noblemen throughout the Nara Period (709–784 A. D.) and the Heian Period (784–1186 A. D.) until in the reign of the Emperor Sutoku (1124–1141 A. D.) twenty linked poems were included in the famous anthology *Kin-yō-shū* (金葉集) or "A Collection of Golden Leaves" which was compiled by Imperial command.

The canons of the short poem being numerous and complicated, those who left it and turned to the linked poem, which was comparatively easier to compose and in which wit could be freely exercised, steadily increased in number; and in the last years of the Heian Period, *kusari renga* (鎖連歌) or "a chain of linked poems" began to be written. As its name suggests, it is a long series of linked poems, running often to "Fifty Hemistichs" (五十韻) and "One Hundred Hemistichs."

In the Kamakura Period (1186–1339 A. D.), during which the short poem reigned supreme in literary circles, the writers of linked poems were divided into two antagonistic groups called respectively *Ushin-ha* (有心派) and *Mushin-ha* (無心派). The *Ushin-ha* or "Refined School" composed linked poems which were serious both in content and language and bore a striking resemblance to the short poem. The *Mushin-ha* or "Unrefined School" attached as great importance to the comic and humorous as their predecessors did; and their poems came to be called *Haikai-no-Renga* or simply *Haikai* (俳諧) or "Comic Linked Poems," the epithet *Haikai* being borrowed from the anthology *Kokin-Shū* (古今集) or "A Collection of Poems, Ancient and Modern." Comic linked poems were often composed as *yokyō* or "after-entertainment" at *renga* parties; and in consequence the *renga* writers at large made light of them, and comic poems waned rapidly. On the other hand, the serious linked poem ultimately gained an undisputed ascendancy; and as had been the case with the short poem, troublesome rules of composition were established now and then until at last they attained to such a number that it became impossible for poets to commit them to memory.

Toward the close of the reign of the Emperor Go-Kōgon (1352–1371) of the Northern Court twenty volumes of chains of linked poems appeared, called The *Tsukuba* Collection (筑波集). The word *Tsukuba* is derived from the name of a mountain referred to in the above-mentioned first linked poem by an aged man and Prince Yamato-takeru-no-Mikoto and is used as a synonym of the linked poem. Nijō Yoshimoto, the compiler of "The *Tsukuba* Collection," who was Prime Minister and a great poet, established many rules of composition for linked poems. Later these rules were often revised and a large number of new rules were added to them.

Then Zenna, Bonna, Sōgi and many other *renga* poets of great merit made their appearance one after another and shone brilliantly in the literary galaxy of the Muromachi Period.

The first hemistich of a chain of linked poems called, *hokku* (發句) or "starting hemistich," must be a complete sentence and contain a word referring to one or other of the four seasons. The *hokku* was the most important of all the hemistichs and had to be composed by the best poet of the joint writers—in most cases a master of linked poems—or by a poet of noble birth. The party was usually made up of from three to five men. There were remarkable exceptions to the rule. For instance, "The *Sarumino* Collection" (猿蓑集) contains a chain of linked poems composed by sixteen writers, including Bashō, Otokuni, Chigetsu, Kyorai and Chinseki. The *hokku* which was later renamed *haiku** (俳句) began to be composed independently of linked poems in the early days of the Muromachi Period (1339–1565); which circumstance can safely be inferred from the fact that some *hokku* are included in "The *Tsukuba* Collection" just mentioned and in "The New *Tsukuba* Collection" compiled by Sōgi (1420–1502).

As has already been seen, the linked poem had come into vogue since the Kamakura Period because the too troublesome canons of the short poem had driven many poets to its cause.

* The name *haiku* is a cross between *hokku* and *haikai.*

But, in course of time, the writers of linked poems in their turn had established much more complicated rules of composition, so that the linked poem was now dull and monotonous in thought and expression. Moreover, the linked poem was nothing but a plaything of the privileged classes. Under the circumstances, naturally enough a reaction set in. The *haikai* or "comic linked poems" which had been eking out a feeble existence sprung up with new vigour and virtually overwhelmed the serious linked poem.

The representatives of the reactionary movement were Yamazaki Sōkan (1465–1553) and Arakida Moritake (1472–1549). In contradistinction to the writers of serious linked poems, they freely used colloquial and even slang expressions, setting at naught the complicated canons, displayed wit and humour of no common degree and often chose their themes from daily affairs. In consequence the *haikai* poem was warmly welcomed by the common people and became popular throughout the empire. In those days none of the *renga* poets could rival these two powerful writers; and thus the *renga* declined gradually until the *haikai* attained supremacy. Sōkan issued a collection of comic linked poems entitled *The Inu Tsukuba Shū* (犬筑波集) or "The Popular *Tsukuba* Collection," the greater majority of the poems being from his own pen. Wit and humour are the keynote of his verses, some of which are spoiled by indecent language. The following are the best known of his verses.

Some one having proposed as a second hemistich the lines:—

I'm willing to kill him—
Unwilling to kill him.

Sōkan immediately added the first hemistich:—

I've caught the thief; alas!
He proves to be my own son.

Snow-man, even though you feel cold,
Do not warm yourself at the fire.

Moritake who was a priest of the Great Ise Shrines and nobler in character, had a more advanced view of poetry. He thought that humour and jest were not everything with *haikai* poets, and sought a purer style. He wrote "One Thousand Hemistichs by Moritake," the first volume of a very large number of *haikai* linked poems. It is his great achievement that, in disregard of the canons of the *renga*, he established a new code for the *haikai* poetry.

The following are typical *hokku* by him:—

On the morning of New Year's Day,
I think even of the Age of Gods.

Fall'n flowers flew back to the branch!
Nay, they were flitting butterflies.

From this time on *hokku* i. e. *haiku*, as an independent form of literature, steadily grew in vogue.

The deaths of Sōkan and Moritake, the promoters and ruling spirits of the *haikai*, proved a great blow to its cause, and the *haikai* continued at a low ebb for about a quarter of a century. At this juncture appeared Matsunaga Teitoku (1570–1653), through whose untiring efforts the *haikai* awakened from its stupor and came into vogue again. Teitoku, a samurai's son, had a propensity for verse-making from childhood. He took lessons in *tanka* composition from Kujō Kyūzan, Hosokawa Yūsai and many other celebrated poets and studied the prosody of *renga* from Satomura Shōha. Thus in his boyhood he thoroughly acquainted himself with the rules of composition of the two types of poetry. In his early manhood he became a votary of *haikai*; and later, on the basis of the canons of the *renga*, he established a new system of *haikai* regulations, which was published in book form entitled The *Go-San** (御傘) or "His Lordship's Umbrella." His style had a slightly retrogressive tendency toward the *renga*; and in his hands, the rules of composition became complicated again. But it is undeniable that he did a great deal in the revival of the *haikai*. He had many able disciples, such as Matsue Shigeyori, Kitamura Kigin and Miyabara Teishitsu, the last named being popularly known as the writer of the verse :—

"Ah, Ah!" was all that I could say
On flower-clad Mount Yoshino.

The revival and great vogue of *haikai* was due largely to the endeavours of these disciples. The Teitoku School aimed chiefly at play on words, such as pivot-words and associated words, and at the display of low wit and pleasantry. Even the verses of Teitoku himself are far from perfection.

Lo! ice and water joyfully
Are reconciled to one another.

---

* In connection with the phrase *sashiai-nashi* equally applicable to a nobleman's umbrella and to versification, which I find it impossible to render into English, the title *Go-San* signifies that with the regulations contained in the book at one's command, one can compose *haikai* poems with correctness.

The cause of all men's midday naps—
The autumn moon.

Just at the time when the pun and the monotonous style of the Teitoku School were beginning to estrange the general public, Nishiyama Sō-in (1604–1682) appeared to throw a new ray of light on the *haikai* world. Sō-in, who was a retainer of Katō Masakata, the lord of the castle of Yatsushiro, in the province of Higo, was thrown out of employment when his lord's family went to ruin. Then he removed to Fushimi near the Imperial capital Kyōto, and later to Ōsaka. He shaved his head and became a Buddhist priest; and leading a sequestered life, devoted himself to the study of poetry. First he wrote verses of the Teitoku Style; but once engaged in writing *haikai*, his progress was wonderful, and he soon became discontented with the monotonous style of the Teitoku School. In due time, he started a new style of his own, and for its propagation travelled extensively through the Sanyōdō provinces, the Ō-u district and Kyūshū Island. Its characteristics consist in the free use of redundant words, in utter disregard of usage, and of a rich vocabulary, whether Chinese words or slang expressions. The following are typical of Sō-in's verses:—

No, no, not even cherry-bloom
Can equal this night's brilliant moon.

The cuckoo is singing;
Ye gods, be sure to listen.

A winter shower falls on the roof;
The valley is deep and I am deaf.

Sō-in's style, which was widely known as the Danrin Style (壇林派), was eagerly welcomed by the public which had grown tired of the Teitoku Style. The appellation, "Danrin School," it may be noted in parenthesis, was adopted from the name of the house of Tashiro Shō-i, one of Sō-in's prominent Yedo disciples, who called his residence the Danrin-Ken. Another circumstance was favourable to the spread of the Danrin Style. In those days, the Tokugawa Government's Confucian policy being in force, society was regulated by the strict teaching of the Chu-Hi doctrines and further by the formalism of the feudal system. The people at large, suffocated in the heavy atmosphere, naturally yearned for freedom in everything. Their reactionary mood contributed something to making them turn to the Danrin School, which afforded great freedom both in subject-matter and language.

Vehement controversies took place with frequency between the votaries of the Danrin and the Teitoku Schools (貞德派), until at last the Danrin School gained a complete victory and threw the rival school into the shade. It was in the ascendant not only in Yedo, Kyōto and Ōsaka, but also throughout the provinces.

Sō-in had a number of excellent disciples, among whom the following are worthy of special notice:—Ihara Saikaku, Shiigamoto Saimaro, Okanishi Ichū, Tashiro Shō-i above-mentioned, who all lived in Ōsaka, and Arai Hakuseki, Naitō Fūko and his son Rosen and Endō Masatomo, all of whom lived in Yedo; and many votaries of the Teitoku School turned Sō-in's disciples.

Now that the Danrin Style had gained the ascendancy, its downward tendency set in. Sō-in's free and irregular prosody led his followers to adopt a loose, chaotic style which became worse and worse until their verses were perfect doggerel. When the Danrin Style was thus at the bottom of the abyss of degeneration, it was Kamijima Onitsura (1660–1738), who infused a new vitality into the *haikai* world.

Onitsura was a native of the town of Itami, in Settsu Province. First he was a *sakê* distiller; later he removed to Ōsaka and turned acupuncturator. Since the *renga* and the *haikai* had been in vogue among his fellow townsfolk for generations, Onitsura took to verse-making at seven or eight almost without knowing it; and when he grew older, he composed *haikai* of the Teitoku Style under the instruction of Matsue Shigeyori. Later, through a thorough analysis of both the Teitoku and the Danrin Styles, he realized that they were an idle pastime. Thereupon he abandoned their verses and seriously thought over the problem, and virtually arrived at the conclusion that, in verse-writing, sincerity of motive was of greater importance than technique—that a literary life and soul was essential to true poetry. Then he did his utmost in metamorphosing into pure literature the *haikai* which hitherto had not advanced a step beyond a literary pastime in the hands of Sōkan, Moritake, Teitoku and Sō-in. In this revolutionary movement he achieved remarkable success, and has left a significant record in the history of *haikai* as a pioneer of the literary *haikai*. Below are typical verses of Onitsura.

Nowhere can I throw away
The bath water,
Insects singing all around.

The waterfowl looks heavy,
Yet lo! it floats on water.

It is to be deplored that Onitsura had only two or three disciples of mediocre talent; in consequence of which, after his death the *haikai* world was monopolized by the disciples of a contemporary of his, the greatest *haikai* poet that Japan has ever produced. It was none but Matsuo Bashō (松尾芭蕉) (1644–1694) who, with his so-called *Shō-fū* or Bashō Style ("Shō" is an abbreviation of Bashō), which is characterized by symbolism, naturalism and quietude and strange to say, subjectivity, brought about a complete revolution of *haikai* poetry. This thorough innovation was achieved just when the Genroku* culture bloomed in its highest glory. In literature, in painting, in sculpture, in drama, and other fields, the Japanese genius attained the most exalted height that was capable of. This period teems with brilliant names—Saikaku** the novelist, Chikamatsu the dramatist, Kada no Azumamaro, the authority on Japanese literature, Kumazawa Banzan, Ogyū Sorai, Itō Jinsai the Confucianists, Ogata Kōrin and Hanabusa Itchō the painters, Yokoya Sōmin the sculptor and so on *ad infinitum*. It is little wonder that, in such an atmosphere, Bashō, the revolutionist of *haikai* poetry, should have made his advent.

In his early twenties, Bashō, a native of Iga Province, went up to Kyōto, and became pupil-servant of Kitamura Kigin, under whose instruction he studied Japanese classics, the *renga* and *haikai*; while on the other hand, he took lessons in Chinese classics from Itō Tan-an. After a few years of close application, he went up to Yedo, and there under adverse circumstances began his career as a *haikai* writer and before long

* "Genroku" (元禄) is the name of the era in which Bashō flourished.

** Saikaku was also a *haikai* poet, as above mentioned, but he was greater as a novelist.

became a master of the art. In 1686 when he was forty-three years of age, he composed his most famouse verse on " The Old Pond," which proved to be the foundation-stone of the Bashō Style. It was really by Bashō that the *haikai* was elevated into pure literature, serious in character, a literature in the true sense of the term. The change was not a retrogression to the *renga* but a remarkable advance. Moreover, not only was he a great genius in verse-making, but also a man of character; which fact contributed greatly to a steady increase of his admirers and pupils. During his extensive pilgrimages through the provinces, extending over eleven years, over two thousand men became his pupils, among whom were to be counted Kikaku, Ransetsu, Kyorai, Sampū and a dozen other prominent poets. The Bashō School eclipsed both the Teitoku and the Danrin Schools, and virtually came to hold an undisputed reign over the *haikai* world. Nay, his style has continued to exercise a great influence through nearly two centuries and a half up to the present day.

In the days of the Teitoku and the Danrin Schools, the linked poem was in greater fashion than the *hokku*, and " One Hundred Hemistichs " was the exclusive form; but Bashō originated the standard set of " Thirty-six Hemistichs " called *Kasen* or " Poetical Geniuses," so named after the celebrated " Six-and-Thirty Poetical Geniuses " of the Heian Period. Furthermore, Bashō and his pupils attached as much importance to *hokku* as to linked poems. To speak more exactly, their *hokku* are about as numerous as their linked poems.

Below are Bashō's typical *hokku* :—

The ancient pond!
A frog plunged—splash!

A crow is perched on a bare branch.
It is an autumn eve.

The sea is wild! The Milky Way extends
Far over to the island of Sado.

Collecting all the rains of May,
How swiftly flows the Mogami!

It is a noteworthy fact that about the Enkyō Era (1744–1748) the *hokku* began often to be called *haiku* and the *haikai*, *renku* (連句) or "linked verses."

Bashō's *haiku* are finished art, giving expression to actual life—an expression of what he calls "a life of *fūga*" or "poetical refinement." It is indeed in his *haiku* and his prose accounts of travels and miscellanies that his poetic genius and his spirit and character are displayed in their true colours. Yes, his *haiku* are his great triumph and his greatness as a poet chiefly lies in them. It is principally in the case of *haiku* that he preached and practised his famous saying *Fu-eki ryūkō* (不易流行) or "eternal truths in nature and human life, and the freshness of expression and technique," and his most important sayings *sabi* or "quietude," *shi-ori* or "rhythmical expression" and *hosomi* or "delicacy." Some of his subjective verses are perfect jewels. Even in the case of objective description, his feelings are infused harmoniously, so that his verses are hardly susceptible of the classification of "subjective" and "objective."

The case is different with his linked verses. It is true they are far superior to his predecessors' verses; yet, since *renku* are essentially joint work by a few writers, even Bashō, with his great genius, could not thoroughly change their traditional nature as a literary pastime. In the case of *haiku*, the writer can do as his subejctive feelings choose, he is under no restraint and enjoys absolute freedom; consequently he can assume an attitude of spontaneous intuition. On the other hand, in the composition of linked verses, the writer is hampered by the previous verse which he is to cap and cannot give free play to his spontaneous impulse of composition. Furthermore, the joint writers of *renku* are different in ability and personality, and quite naturally, the manner of joining and content are different in different verses, the resultant whole being locally different in merit. The lack of unity in the theme is another characteristic, which, however, is considered rather the essence and interest of *renku*. The theme gradually changes in one verse after another, in such a manner that the theme treated of in the first verse is quite different from that treated of in the last verse. To give a concrete instance. First the cherry-blossom is talked of; next the subject-matter changes to Koganei, a place noted for cherry-thees, then to the Tama River from which the Koganei canal is conducted, next to the fishing of *ayu* (a kind of river trout) in the river, whence the scene is changed to the cormorant-fishing of *ayu* on the Nagara River, next to the castle of Gifu and so on *ad infinitum*. This gradual, almost imperceptible change of the theme is the most important feature of *renku*. After all, a chain of linked verses is a piece of patchwork, a compromise arranged by several writers. Therefore, Bashō's attitude when joining a *renku* party is naturally different from that he assumes as a *haiku* poet; his attitude is less serious, his mood is more humorous. However, it is a point quite worthy of Bashō that he set free *renku* writers from many of the traditional regulations and gave them ample latitude for the free play of their ability. For instance, it had been one of those rules that the *hokku* of the linked verses should be written by a man of high birth or by a master of poetry; but this usage was not always observed by the Bashō School.

Bashō confesses, "Among my disciples are many good writers of *hokku*, but I seem to have a knack of writing *haikai*." By *haikai* he means *renku*. Judging from this remark, he had strong self-confidence in writing *renku* and really he had uncommon ability as a *renku* writer, and did a great deal in ridding the *renku* from plays on words, low wit and vulgar language. Moreover, Bashō discarded the time-honoured usage of joining verses by the relationship of content and of words, and originated a new process by taking into consideration what he calls *utsuri* or "smooth transition," *hibiki* or "vibrations," *nioi* or "odour," *kurai* or "dignity": that is, he aimed at keeping up harmony between verses in taste and dignity. Again, he infused into the *renku* his all-important principle of quietude. Thus, in his hands, the *renku* became much more refined than it had hitherto been, not only in language but also in content and achieved a remarkable approach toward pure literature.

During Bashō's lifetime, in spite of diversity in their personality and manner of life, his disciples' art, influenced by his art and character, and polished and selected by his criticism, constituted the Bashō Style. But after his death, the absence of his great influence gave birth to the rampant outpourings of their unrestrained inclinations. Although the keynote of their verses still remained the Bashō Style, their respective characteristics differentiated steadily, and the gap between them widened as time went on; and the styles of those of them who respectively became centres of influence, were, without exception, of bad tendencies and rapidly went from bad to worse. About half a century of degeneration and stagnation followed down to the Tenmei era when appeared Taniguchi (or Yosano) Buson (1715–1783), a great genius, who effected the "Revival of the Tenmei Era."

A native of a village near Ōsaka, Buson was passionately fond of painting from his childhood and in his later years originated the Yosano Style, a harmony of the Northern and Southern Schools of Chinese painting. At Yedo he studied the *haikai* under Uchida Tenzan and Hayano Hajin. Afterwards he became a master of *haikai*, contributed a great deal to the restoration of the Bashō Style and succeeded also in building up a new style of his own. He had a large number of pupils, including good poets such as Kitō, Shōha, Gekkyo, Tōkō and Hyakuchi.

Buson's style is different from Bashō's in some respects. While Bashō selected for his themes mainly natural beauties apart from human life, Buson eagerly welcomed human affairs as well as natural beauties. Most of Bashō's verses are based on his own experiences and have the advantage of a powerful impressiveness; but Buson, who had a strong inclination towards classicism, wrote many verses on romantic themes borrowed from Japanese and Chinese classics, or on interesting incidents in history, giving free play to fantasy and imagination. While Bashō has a deep insight into the essence of things, Buson excels in the delineation of minute parts of things and in exact observation and in skilful description. In a word, Buson's characteristics are variety of subject-matter, minuteness of observation and great skill in expression. Another feature is a wonderful realism and a vivid descriptive power derived from his style of painting. Many of his verses are sketches in words. In this respect he is unparalleled.

Below are typical verses of Buson.

Upon the temple-bell
A butterfly is sleeping well.

Lo! in spring rain an umbrella
Walks chatting with a straw rain-coat.

What an expanse of rape flowers,
With the moon east and the sun west!

The peony flowers having scattered,
A few petals lie one on another.

There is a feature in the *haikai* of the Buson period which must not be lost sight of—a humorous tendency which has something in common with the humorous essays and fiction which had come into vogue then. The most playful poets are Yayū and Ō-emaru whose verses are far distant from Bashō's verses.

Over departed Spring
None cries so loud as frogs. By Yayū

The beans at its feet are stolen,
Yet quite unaware—the scarecrow. Ditto

It is the Happy New Year's Day;
I was not such an old daddy after all. By Ō-emaru

If butterflies danced through the falling snow,
I wonder what a sight it would be! Ditto

Issa (1762–1827) is apt to be thought a humorous poet of the same tendency; but it is a superficial view to consider him such. He is far from being such a poet. It is true that in his verses love and its direct opposite, hatred—the love of the weaker and the hatred of the stronger—are clad in the dress of humour; and his language, full of slang, often excites the comic sense. But Issa's verses are essentially pathetic; his is often a tragic art on human life. They are poems on human affairs dressed in *haikai*.

Under cherry-flowers,
None are utter strangers. **By Issa**

Alas! in my old home,
Even flies sting men! **Ditto**

What a beautiful kite
Is flying from
A beggar's hovel! **Ditto**

Ours is a world of suffering,
Even if cherry-flowers bloom. **Ditto**

The cherry-blossoms forced
A daimio to dismount. **Ditto**

After Issa's days the *haikai* world at large again took a downward trend—a shallow imitation of the Buson Style—and the vulgarization of taste went on as time passed. Over half a century of degeneration passed before Masaoka Shiki (1868–1902) achieved the second revival of *haikai*. With a sound judgment based on new principles of criticism then prevalent, he first found out the merits of Bashō and next discovered Buson's art which he admired to the verge of worship. The most distinguishing feature of his verses is a vivid realism which is not inferior to Buson's realism. But it is greatly to be regretted that Shiki did not take a single step beyond realism, and in consequence his movement remained one-sided. But for his premature death, with his brilliant genius, he might have advanced further and virtually attained the height of Buson, nay even of Bashō.

How the skylark soars,
Treading on the cloud,
Inhaling the haze! By Shiki

How fast the Mogami River
Washes away the hot summer! Ditto

The sun and moon are staring fierce
At each other in east and west. Ditto

At the present day, Kyoshi (1974–), the most prominent disciple of Shiki, and a realistic poet, is the greatest *haiku* writer; and among other numerous poets, these are worthy of notice:—Kubutsu, Hekigotō, Seisensui, Kijō, Seisei, Bushi, Seihō, Getto, Shichō, Bakujin, Sekitei and Kyokō. Seisensui maintains that reference to a season of the year is not a necessary element in *haiku* and composes irregular verses, often fewer and sometimes more than the traditional seventeen syllables; and Hekigotō writes long verses consisting often of over twenty syllables and unintelligible to the uninitiated.

It is a noteworthy fact that during the last half century

very few poets have written *renku* and it may safely be said that the *renku* is at present an almost extinct art and there are no signs of its revival. The decline of the *renku* is largely to be attributed to the fact that Shiki maintained that the *renku* is not literature and did not essay his hand in this direction.

Behold! the spring moon paints
Pictures on the high waves. By Kyoshi

How heavily rain pours down on
The hat I stole from a scarecrow! Ditto

A baby which gazes at falling flowers,
With its mouth open, is a Buddha. By Kubutsu

III

A Sketch of Bashō (芭蕉)

Bashō (芭蕉) was born in the year 1644 at the castle-town Ueno, the capital of the province of Iga. The month and the day of his birth are quite unknown. His father, Matsuo Gizaemon, was a samurai of lower rank. Gizaemon had three sons: the eldest son, Yazaemon, was a teacher of penmanship, the second son, Hanzaemon, succeeded to the father's estate and the youngest son was Bashō.

Bashō's given name was Jinshichirō (甚七郎) and "Bashō" was the *nom de plume* he assumed in his later years. At the age of nine Jinshichirō, a sagacious boy, was made page to Yoshitada, eldest son of Tōdō Shinshirō who was in charge of the castle of Ueno. Yoshitada, who had some literary propensity, studied *waka** from the Reizei family and *haikai* from Kitamura Kigin, a poet of the Teitoku School, and his pen name was Sengin (蟬吟) (lit. "The Song of Cicadas"). As messenger of his lord, Jinshichirō often called on Kigin who resided in Kyōto, the Imperial capital. Under these circumstances, the young samurai unconsciously came to cultivate a taste for the *haikai* of the Teitoku School: and it is said that at the age of fourteen, he composed a humorous verse characteristic of the school. The accomplished Sengin was at once his lord and his teacher of poetry. Lord and retainer composed linked poems

* *Waka* is a general term for *tanka* or "short poems" consisting of thirty-one syllables and *chōka* or "long poems" three or four, sometimes seven or eight times as long as *tanka.*

now and then; and Jinshichirō's progress in poetry was so remarkable that in his twenty-second year several verses from his pen together with Sengin's verses were included in an anthology edited by the then famous poet Ogino Ansei.

Thus sharing the same literary taste, Jinshichirō and Sengin entertained a particular fondness toward each other. Let it be mentioned *en passant* that about this time Jinshichirō changed his name to Munefusa (宗房).

When Munefusa was twenty-three, Sengin, his lord, his companion and his friend, died suddenly to his profound sorrow; and the transitoriness of life powerfully affected the young samurai. He went sorrowfully up to Mount Kōya with a lock of the deceased's hair, to deposit it in the great Buddhist monastery thereon. The grief-stricken Munefusa, tradition says, was seized with a sudden desire to renounce the world. In July of the same year, despite his relatives' and comrades' remonstrances, he deserted his lord's house. But his desertion seems to have had nothing to do with his pessimistic view of life, some scholars going so far as to aver that he fled lest an intrigue with his dead lord's young wife might be brought to light. Previous to his departure, Munefusa is said to have nailed the following verse on the gate-post of his colleague Jō Magotayū:—

Kumo to hedatsu
Tomo kaya kari no
Ikiwakare

I am now to separate from my comrades,
As wild geese parted by clouds from one another.

After his flight, Munefusa went to Kyōto, where he became pupil-servant of Kigin, under whose instruction he studied Japanese classics, the *renga* and the *haikai* of the Teitoku School, whilst, on the other hand, he took lessons in Chinese classics from Itō Tan-an, a famous authority on the subject. During these years Munefusa, out of his passionate admiration of the Chinese poet Li Pai (李白), which name signifies " The White Damson," assumed the pen name of Tōsei (桃青) which means " The Green Peach." While devoting himself to the study of Japanese and Chinese classics and prosody, he assiduously wrote verses, and that his poetic talent was already recognized by Kyōto poets is to be inferred from the fact that some of his verses were inserted in a collection of *haikai* verses edited by Tanaka Jōkyo, a well known poet.

In September, 1672, when his teacher Kigin removed to Yedo at the Shōgun's summons, Tōsei also went to the Shōgun's capital; where he lived for some time with Ogawa Bokuseki, an Yedo man who had been his fellow-student under Kigin. To earn his living he sought employment, and through the good offices of Bokuseki, obtained the position of a superintendent over the construction of water-supply works at Sekiguchi, Koishikawa. He was then thirty years old. Even while busily engaged in official duties, he continued to study the classics and to compose verses. Soon afterward Tōsei resigned, probably because the employment did not suit him. Then he started his career as a teacher of *haikai* prosody and during two or three years struggled for a bare existence. It was during these years that Enomoto Kikaku, a stripling of fourteen years, destined in later years to become the greatest of Bashō's Ten

Great Disciples, became his pupil. In 1677 was issued "Two Hundred Hemistichs On Spring," linked poems which Tōsei had written jointly with Yamaguchi Sodō and Itō Shintoku, good poets. It was followed the next year by "Three Yedo Poets' Verses" by the same poets. About this time, at the kind proposal of his pupil, Sugiyama Sampū, Tōsei took up residence in a hut belonging to the latter, situated on the left bank of the Sumida River, at Rokkenbori, in Fukagawa. Sampū was a rich fish-purveyor to the Shōgun's household; and the hut in question, which is said to have consisted of one room of six or eight mats, had been originally the lodge of a watchman of the fish-pond. Possessed of a remarkable literary taste he was an ardent admirer of Tōsei; and the poet lived upon the assistance of Sampū and other pupils who increased in number year after year. The poet planted a banana-tree ("bashō") in the garden, and his pupils called his cottage "Bashō-An" (芭蕉庵) or "Banana Hermitage." Accordingly he assumed the pen name of "Bashō." He shaved his head and dressed himself in priestly garb, although he was not ordained, as was the custom with a master of *haikai* poetry. About that time Bashō studied the doctrines of the Zen sect of Buddhism under Abbot Butchō, a man of virtue and attainment, the chief priest of a temple at Kashima, Shimōsa Province, who happened then to be sojourning in his neighbourhood. Also he took lessons in the same subject from Hankei, a famous Zen priest; and it is hardly necessary to say that these studies profoundly influenced his views of life, his mode of living and his verses, both in style and content. Until about 1678 Bashō was a poet of the Danrin School as may well be inferred from the contents of "Two Hundred Hemistichs On Spring." Three years later in 1681, his epoch-making verse appeared in "The Azuma Diary" —

Kare-eda ni
Karasu no tomaritaruya
Aki no kure

A crow is perched on a bare branch;
It is an autumn eve.

Sodō, his friend and a good poet above mentioned, capped this verse as follows :—

Kuwa katage yuku
Kiri no tōzato

A peasant walks shouldering a hoe
In a distant village in mist.

Bashō's verse slightly altered reappeared in "The Round Fan of Autumn," issued in 1864, and again in "The Wilderness," issued in 1689 :—

Kare-eda ni
Karasu no tomari keri
Aki no kure

As is to be readily noticed, *tomaritaruya* was changed to *tomarikeri,* which is the same in meaning but sounds more smoothly.

The solitary crow on a leafless bough which seems typically to symbolize the dreariness of life must have also symbolized the poet's frame of mind. His *haikai* which had hitherto been verses of the lips and of imitation had now become verses of the mind and of originality. It may safely be said that Bashō's characteristic style—a serious, quiet, refined and naturalistic style which he and his disciples called *Shōfū** or the "Bashō Style" or the "Legitimate Style"—dates from the above verse which Bashō composed when he was thirty-seven years of age. Already a fair number of excellent poets was now found among his pupils, such as Kikaku, Ransetsu, Sampū, Sora, who were destined later to shine brilliantly in the galaxy of the Bashō School.

In the winter of 1682 a great fire occurred in Yedo, and unfortunately the Banana Hermitage fell a victim to the flames. Bashō had a narrow escape and took refuge in the house of Sampū's elder sister in the province of Kai, where he stayed for some months. The conflagration which had reduced to ashes the greater part of the metropolis in a few hours made the poet keenly realize the vanity of life and human impotency. In May of the following year, in compliance with his pupils' earnest request, he came back to Yedo. In September through their subscriptions, his hut was reconstructed and a banana tree was planted in its garden. Bashō's reputation rose as the days went on, and his pupils steadily increased, but he was not content with staying all the time in Yedo. Bashō, who idolized and emulated the wandering Chinese poets, Li Pai (李白) (A. D. 705–762) and Tu Fu (杜甫) (A. D. 712–770), and the itinerant Japanese poets, Saigyō (西行) and Sōgi (宗祇), eagerly desired to make a pilgrimage through the Empire, for the twofold purpose of visiting natural beauties and historic scenes for

---

* *Shō* is represented either by the Chinese character signifying *Shō* (蕉), an abbreviation of "Bashō," or by *Shō* (正) signifying "legitimate."

poetic inspiration and of conversing with poetic friends in the provinces for the spread of his doctrines of poetry.

Accordingly, accompanied by his pupil Chiri, a native of Yamato Province, he started on his first pilgrimage in August, 1684, when he was forty years of age. It is interesting here to note his singular travelling garb. He wore a large basket-work hat, paper-clothes* and a light-brown cotton coat, with a scrip round his neck, carrying in hand a walking stick and a rosary of one hundred and eight beads; the scrip contained two or three anthologies, Chinese and Japanese, a flute and a tiny wooden gong. In a word he looked like a Buddhist pilgrim. Touring many a day along the Tōkaidō Highway, Bashō and his companion went to the province of Ise where they worshipped at the Great Temples.** Then taking their way northward, they found themselves in September at Bashō's old home at Ueno, where the poet was re-united to his brother Hanzaemon after sixteen long years' separation. It may well be imagined that their joy knew no bounds; but at the same time, Bashō must have burst into tears to remember that his parents had passed away during his absence. It may be said in this connection that, as far as my knowledge goes, nothing is known about his eldest brother Yozaemon in those days. After some days' stay the two proceeded to the province of Yamato, where they parted company, Chiri returning home to his house in that province. Next Bashō, making a pilgrimage

---

* *Kamiko* (紙衣) or "paper clothes" were made of pure Japanese paper, soft and tough, and worn generally by poor people.

** The Great Temples of Ise are the most sacred of all Shintō temples, dedicated to the Sun-Goddess Tenshōkō Daijin, ancestress of the Emperors, and to the Goddess of Food, Toyoke Daijin.

through the provinces of Mino and Owari, re-visited Ueno, at the close of December, where he bade the old year farewell and hailed the new year. In January he left his old home, and after travelling solitarily and verse-making through the provinces of Yamato, Yamashiro, Ōmi, Owari and Kai, came back to the Banana Hermitage late in April. It is noteworthy that during his long tour wherever the poet stopped *haikai* writers of the place called on him to hold a poetry party and most of them became his pupils. Thus this journey contributed a great deal to spreading the Bashō Style through the provinces he had visited. Bashō's delicate health and his long pilgrimage had caused his Yedo pupils and friends no little anxiety, so that his safe return made them heave a profound sigh of relief. The account of the trip in question is entitled the *No-zarashi-Kikō* or "An Account of a Weather-Beaten Trip."

The rest of the year Bashō spent at his hut and the next New Year also he hailed quietly there. It was indeed in this year—1687—when he was forty-three, that he powerfully demonstrated his poetic attitude—that he belonged no longer either to the Teitoku School or to the Danrin School, but was a poet of his own style. In the autumn of the year the *Haru-no-Hi* or "The Spring Days," a collection of his own and his pupils' verses, was issued, in which was inserted his most famous verse:—

Furuike ya
Kawazu tobikomu
Mizu no oto

The ancient pond!
A frog plunged—splash!

During his journey in 1684, at the city of Nagoya, Yamamoto Kakei, Minami Tokoku, Okada Yasui and a few other poets of ability had become Bashō's pupils. With these pupils he had composed " linked verses " which had been issued under the title of the *Fuyu-no-Hi* or " The Winter Days." A comparison of the new volume, " The Spring Days," with " The Winter Days " clearly shows that the poets of the Bashō School had gradually abandoned low wit and puns and had come seriously to observe nature and human life and made remarkable progress in the portrayal of nature. Particularly the above tiny verse on the old pond is an ideal naturalistic poem combining quietude, mysticism and profundity, in which the poet's soul is identified with nature. It is true that judged by present day standards of criticism this verse cannot be called a masterpiece of paramount merit; but it is undeniable that it is an epoch-making verse which is entirely different from the verses of his contemporary poets in being a naturalistic, objective and at the same time, symbolic description of a natural incident. It is no exaggeration to say that the publication of this verse marks the firm establishment of Bashō's characteristic style.

On the bright moonlight night of August 15th, 1687, Bashō's disciples, Kikaku and Sempoku, called at his hut and invited him to hold a moon-viewing party on the Sumida River. The full moon of August 15th of the lunar calendar, i.e. about September 15th, is in Japan the most beautiful of all the full moons, due to the particularly clear autumnal atmosphere; and the harvest moon is so highly appreciated by Japanese poets that when they mention simply " the moon " in verses it means the harvest moon. Presently Bashō and his disciples put off in a boat; but the river was alive with dozens of boats full of moon-viewing people, who made merry, singing aloud over wine or playing the *samisen*.* Therefore the poets rowed down to a quiet part, where they enjoyed the moonlight, drinking and musing on the beautiful sight. Then to their surprise, Sempoku's attendant, while warming *sakê*, burst into the verse:—

Behold! the boat is gliding on
The harvest moon laid on the waves.

The company stayed on far into the night but none was inspired with a line. Coming back to his hut, Bashō strolled round the pond gazing up at the moon, when the following verse flashed across his mind:—

Meigetsu ya
Ike wo meguri te
Yomosugara

What a bright moon! I strolled
Around the pond all night.

Two or three days later Bashō, with whom it was a passion to view the harvest moon, attended by his pupils, Sora and Sōha, left for Kashima, the so-called "Water Town" on the Kita-ura Lagoon which is noted for moon-viewing. They went to Kashima principally by boat on the great Tone River. On their way on board they enjoyed the brilliant moonlight to their hearts' content, but at their destination, to their disappointment, the moon was hidden by clouds. Calling on Abbot Butchō, Bashō's teacher of the Zen sect of Buddhism, at his temple at the town and visiting Itago, another famous "water town," they

* A Japanese banjo-like instrument of three strings.

returned home to Yedo at the end of the month. The account of this journey is called " A Trip to Kashima."

Late in October of the same year, Bashō set out for another journey. Now Sōin, the founder of the Danrin School, was dead; Bashō's reputation had spread throughout the length and breadth of Japan, and his literary friends and pupils in the provinces had earnestly begged him to make a poetic trip. But the present journey was prompted chiefly by his own yearnings. The account of this tour is called " A Trip to Yoshino," because his longings centred mostly in Yoshino, celebrated for the supreme beauty of its cherry-blossoms and for its historic associations. First of all, the poet visited different noted places in the provinces of Owari and Mikawa; and in December went back to his old home where he spent a few happy weeks with his relatives. During these weeks Yoshinaga, his dead lord Sengin's son, held a cherry-viewing party in his honour. Then Bashō burst into the verse:—

Samazama no
Koto omoidasu
Sakurakana

Ah! the cherry-blossoms
Bring back many memories.

In February, 1688, attended by his pupils Sōmu and Sōshichi, our poet went and worshipped at the Great Temples of Ise; and in the middle of March, with his favourite pupil Tokoku, he made a pilgrimage to places of interest in the provinces of Yamato and Kii. At Kōya and Wakano-ura he was particularly favoured by the Muse; but at Yoshino, where they stayed three days, strange to say, Bashō was too much smitten by the natural beauty and the historic interest to compose verses. Nay, to speak more exactly, a legion of excellent verses had been written by ancient poets so that nothing was left for him to say. In April he strolled about the beautiful seaside resorts Suma and Akashi, which are often alluded to in classic poetry and are noted for the decisive battle between the Minamoto and Taira families. During the succeeding three months, he travelled through Ōmi, Mino and Owari; whence, early in August, in company with Etsujin, his Nagoya pupil, he went up Mount Obasute in Shinano Province, celebrated for its view of the harvest moon. Then after paying a visit to the famous Buddhist temple Zenkōji, Bashō returned to Yedo in September. The account of his trip to Mount Obasute is entitled "A Trip to Sarashina," Sarashina being the name of the county in which stands the hill in question.

In March, 1689, accompanied by his pupil Sora, Bashō started on another journey, the longest of all his trips, extending over one hundred and sixty days, which is embodied in his most famous prose writing entitled *Oku-no-Hosomichi* or "A Narrow Pass Through Ōshū," "Oku," being an abbreviation of "Michinoku" or "Ōshū." Bashō wrote five accounts of travels—all masterpieces of the kind, mirroring his character well. "A Narrow Pass Through Ōshū" is the best of them and most characteristic of his prose. Taking their way along the Ōu Highway, they went up to Nikkō, which is both naturally and artificially so magnificent that a popular proverb says "Don't say 'kekkō' (i. e. 'splendid') until you have seen Nikkō." Thence by way of Nasuno-ga-hara Plain, Shirakawa and Fukushima, they found themselves at Sendai, the castle-town of

Lord Date. Next they boated through the pine-clad Matsushima Islets in the Bay of Sendai, one of the "Three Most Beautiful Scenes" of the empire. Bashō was struck with the beauty of the islets, but to his regret, he was inspired with no line, as had been the case at Yoshino. Then they visited the ruins of Hiraizumi where the Fujiwara generals had once achieved glories and Yoshitsune and his loyal retainers had died a most heroic death. It was here that Bashō burst into his famous verse :—

Natsugusa ya
Tsuwamono domo ga
Yume no ato

Ah! summer grasses wave!
The warriors' brave deeds were a dream.

Then trudging along the course of the Kitakami River, they reached Mogami, whence they visited the Ryūshakuji Temple and climbed Mount Haguro. From the town of Tsuruoka, they walked along the Mogami River down to the estuary port Sakata, whence they turned northward along the seashore and went to the town of Kisagata, which is said by the poet to be as beautiful as the Matsushima Islets. Now retracing their steps, they travelled through the provinces of Echigo, Etchū and Kaga. In the last named province Sora was taken ill and, parting company with Bashō, hastened to the house of a friend in the province of Ise. It is said that at Naoetsu in Echigo Province, they asked for a night's lodging at a Buddhist temple, but the priest, looking at their shabby attire, refused their request. So they slept under the eaves of the temple. In

September Bashō reached the town of Ōgaki, in the province of Mino, where he put up at the house of his pupil, Jokō, to take a rest from the fatigue of the long journey. It is needless to say that this trip profoundly influenced Bashō's poetic ideas and contributed greatly to the finish of his style. At Ōgaki, Bashō was heartily welcomed by many pupils. They held poetry parties in his honour, so that he could hardly find time for a complete rest. Early in the same month, he left for Ise to witness the ceremonies of removal of the Great Temples. He went to Yamada by boat on the Ibigawa, but to his disappointment, the ceremonies of the "Inner Temple" were over and he was barely in time to witness the ceremonies of the "Outer Temple." Let it be mentioned in passing that the Temples, which are built entirely of wood, are reconstructed every twenty years when solemn and impressive ceremonies of removal are held. From Yamada, by way of Iga Province, Bashō visited Nara and the then Imperial capital, Kyōto, where he called on his pupil, Kyorai, at his villa Rakushisha at Saga; and spent the year-end at Zeze, a castle-town of Ōmi Province.

Early in the following year Bashō made a pilgrimage again through Ise, Iga and Ōmi; and in April settled down at a cottage close to the shore of the beautiful Lake Biwa in Ōmi. The cottage belonging to his pupil, Suganuma Kyokusui, which had been long left desolate, was repaired on purpose for the sake of the poet, who was passionately fond of the views of the lake. The hut had been the residence of Kyokusui's uncle Genjū, a Buddhist priest, hence its name "Genjū-An" or "Genjū's Cottage." Freely translated, the name of the hut signifies "Ephemeral Life Hermittage"; and Bashō, who highly appreciated Kyokusui's hospitality and enjoyed his sojourn in the cottage, has left a beautiful description of it. In the spring of the same year the *Sarumino-Shū* or "The Monkey's Straw Rain-Coat," the best and most authoritative of the verse collections of the Bashō School, was edited by Kyorai and Bonchō at the master's command. It is a noteworthy fact that Kamijima Onitsura, a great *haikai* poet, then as famous as Bashō, paid him homage in September and they exchanged views on the *haikai*. In 1691 Bashō removed to Kyorai's villa Rakushisha in the vicinity of Kyōto, where he stayed for some months, and then making a pilgrimage through Ōmi, Mino, Owari and Mikawa, came back to Yedo in November. Inasmuch as the "Banana Hermitage" had been handed over to another man just before his departure for the Ōu journey, Bashō passed the close of the year at a temporary residence at Tachibanachō on the right bank of the Sumida River. In the summer of the following year, close to his old hut, a cottage was built for Bashō through the subscriptions of his pupils, and five banana-trees were planted by it. It was again called "The Banana Hermitage," and the poet resided in it during the following two years.

By this time, the Bashō Style had attained the zenith of its vogue, and Bashō was at the height of fame, having numerous pupils all over Japan. A collection of verses of his school was published year after year; and the so-called "The Seven Books of the Bashō School," including "The Winter Days," "The Spring Days," "The Wilderness" and "The Monkey's Straw Rain-Coat," were brought out one after another in the few years we have just spoken of.

On May 11th, 1694, Bashō left for a pilgrimage through

the western provinces. After spending two or three days each at the houses of several pupils residing on the route of the Tōkaidō, he went back to his old home at Ueno in July, where he stayed for weeks. In September he went to Nara, and it was on the 9th of the month that he found himself at Ōsaka, the greatest centre of commerce. There, at the request of many people, he held poetry parties at several places. But it must be remembered that Ōsaka was where the Danrin School had risen and flourished. It is true there were many followers of the Bashō School, but very few of them realized the full significance of his style. It was at a poetry party held at a certain tea-house in the suburbs of the city that he composed the following verse:—

Kono michi ya
Yukuhito nashi ni
Aki no kure

None goes along this way
But I, this autumn eve.

This poem, it may well be imagined, gives vent to his sentiment of loneliness and his disappointment about his Ōsaka pupils.

On the 29th of the month, Bashō held a poetry party at the residence of Madame Sono, a zealous pupil, who gave a sumptuous feast in his honour. Unfortunately the dinner proved fatal to the poet, who had been suffering from indigestion for some days. Probably owing to his overeating mushrooms, he had severe pain that night. A patent medicine was of no avail and the illness, probably dysentery, became more and more serious. The bedridden poet said, "Mokusetsu of Ōtsu knows the usual state of my health very well. Send for him." So the poet-physician came and treated him. Again he said, "I want to speak to Kyorai about something." So Kyorai was sent for from Kyōto. The house of his pupil, Shidō, at which Bashō had been staying since his arrival in Ōsaka, being inconvenient for nursing him, he was removed on October 3 to the back parlour of the house of a florist named Nizaemon, at Minami-Kyūtarō Machi, Midō-mae. Not to speak of Shikō and Izen, who had accompanied the poet in the last journey, Shidō, Kyorai, Mokusetsu, Shara, Donshū, Jōsō, Otokuni and Seishū, who had hurried hither at the news of his illness, nursed him night and day. The alarming tidings spreading through the adjacent provinces, pupils and friends came flocking, full of anxiety and fear. The above mentioned ten pupils received and thanked them, but showed none into the sick-room. Noticing the critical condition of the illness, Mokusetsu suggested to Bashō to send for some other physician, but the dying poet would not listen to the advice, saying, "No, I am quite satisfied with your treatment. I need no other assistance." Asked for a death-verse, he answered, "Well, yesterday's verse is to-day's death-verse. To-day's verse will be to-morrow's death-verse. All the verses I have written through my life—each of them is my death-verse." However, on the 8th, he called to his bedside Jōsō, Kyorai and Donshū and dictated to Donshū the following verse :—

Tabi ni yande
Yume wa kareno wo
Kakemeguru

I'm taken ill while travelling,
And my dreams roam o'er withered moors.

" This is not my death-verse," said the poet " nor is it not my death-verse. At any rate it is a verse suggested by my illness. But to think of such a matter now that I face the great question of life and death, although it is an art to which I have devoted all my life—it may well be called a delusion."

On the 11th, there was an unexpected call from Kikaku of Yedo, who happened to be travelling about the neighbourhood of Ōsaka and had had no knowledge of his master's illness. Master and pupil wept both for joy and sorrow. On the following day, when the last moments were drawing near, Bashō ordered a bath and calling to his beside Kikaku, Kyorai, Jōsō, Otokuni and Seishū, dictated to Shikō and Izen a detailed will about his belongings, with messages to his pupils and servant at Yedo and about his verses and so forth; and wrote himself a note to his brother Hanzaemon at Ueno. Then having said everything he wanted to say, he clasped his hands together and, reciting in murmurs what sounded like a passage of the Kwannon scripture, breathed his last peacefully a little past 4 o'clock, at the age of fifty-one.

On the following day, i. e. the 13th, his remains were conveyed to the town of Ōtsu on Lake Biwa and interred on the 14th in the precincts of the Gichūji Temple situated in its suburbs. A moss-covered tombstone with the simple inscription of *Bashō Ō* or " Master Bashō " penned by Kikaku or Jōsō is still to be seen to the right of the tombstone of General Yoshinaka to whose spirit the temple is dedicated and after whom it is called, *Gichū* being the Chinese pronunciation of the Chinese characters representing "Yoshinaka." Bashō had spent the winter of 1690 at the *Mumei-An* or "The Nameless Hermitage," the living quarters of the temple; and this hut standing on the beautiful lake struck his fancy, for which reason his pupils selected this spot for his resting-place.

Those of the poet's pupils who burned incense before the catafalque were forty; other people whose names were registered in the mourners' book numbered three hundred, and those who attended the funeral without telling their names were countless.

Bashō was a slender and small-statured man, with a thin, fair face, with thick eyebrows and a prominent nose. He had delicate health and suffered from indigestion all his life. It is to be inferred from his letters that he was quiet, modest, scrupulously careful, large-hearted, and faithful to his relatives and friends. He loved his immediate pupils as if they had been his own children, and they, on their part, served him with a sort of filial piety. Although he suffered from poverty all his life and lived half his life on his pupils' sustenance, he was quite indifferent to poverty and always maintained a calm and easy mood.

Bashō left no children, having led a life of celibacy. It is said that during his days at the "Banana Hermitage" he kept a concubine and his young servant Jirobei was his son; but this is a matter of conjecture. His brother, Hanzaemon, died after him, but nothing is known of his eldest brother and their descendants. Tradition says that his pupils all over Japan were more than two thousand, among whom were found some three hundred good poets who were dispersed chiefly in Yedo, Ōsaka and Kyōto and in the provinces of Owari, Mino, Ōmi,

Iga, Kaga, Ise and Shinano, each exerting his influence in spreading the poet's teachings. This immense influence of Bashō is due, it is true, to his wonderful poetic genius, but his excellent character undeniably contributed something toward it.

A Portrait Of Bashō

By Buson

Classic Haiku

The Pre-Bashō Period (Approximately, from the middle of the 15th century to the middle of the 17th century)

宗　鑑（姓一山崎）
天文十五年歿　享年八十九

Sōkan (surname, Yamazaki)
A native of Ōmi Province; page to Shōgun Ashikaga Yoshihisa, later led a hermit's life (1458–1546)

[1]

富　士　山

元日の　見るものにせむ　富士の山　　宗　鑑

Fuji-san

Gwanjitsu no
Miru-mono ni sen
Fuji-no-yama

Mount Fuji

I would keep peerless Mount Fuji
A special sight for New Year's Day.　　Sōkan

On New Year's Day, which is in Japan the most sacred day in all the year, we feel holy and are free from foul thoughts. In consequence everything we see and hear seems to have something pure and dignified about it. In particular is this the case with the snow-capped Mount Fuji. The poet thinks that this peerlessly beautiful and sacred mountain is the most fitting sight for the holiest day. Of the verses of Sōkan who was, together with Moritake, the founder of *haikai*, this piece is the best known; and taking into consideration the condition of the *haikai* in this period, it is worth notice as an embodiment of some steps taken toward literary *haikai*.

守　武 (姓一荒木田)
天文十八年歿　享年七十七
Moritake (surname, Arakida)
A high priest of the Great Ise
Shrines (1472–1549)

[2]

元　　朝

元朝や　神代の事も　思はるゝ

守　武

Gwanchō

Gwanchō ya
Kamiyo no koto mo
Omowaruru

New Year's Day

On the morning of New Year's Day,
I think even of the Age of Gods.

Moritake

On the morning of the very first day of the New Year the poet first of all thinks of the pre-historic Age of Gods. It is quite natural that Moritake, a high priest of the Great Shrines of Ise, should have such a pious mood on the most divine day. It may safely be said that this verse, as well known as Sōkan's verse on Mount Fuji, is one of those typical poems which represent the transition period toward Bashō.

[3]

胡　　蝶

落花枝に 歸ると見れば 胡蝶かな

守　武

Kochō

Rakka eda ni
Kaeru to mireba
Kochō kana

A Butterfly

A fallen flower flew back to the branch!
Behold! it was a flitting butterfly.

Moritake

The spring was advanced and fallen flowers were fluttering down to the ground. Behold! one of them fluttered up again to the branch from which it had fallen. No, it was an illusion. Looking carefully, it proved to be a beautiful white butterfly. What a beautiful sight in the departing spring! This tiny verse well expresses the poet's regrets for fallen flowers.

* * * * *

Fall'n flow'r returning to the branch—
Behold! it is a butterfly.

Trans. by Basil Hall Chamberlain

I thought I saw the fallen *leaves*
Returning to their branches;
Alas, butterflies were they.

Trans. by Yone Noguchi

I thought: back to their branch
The fallen flowers float and rise.
I looked again—lo! 'twas the butterflies.

Trans. by Curtis Hidden Page

Where the soft drifts lie
Of fallen blossoms, dying,
Did one flutter now,
From earth to its own brown bough?
Ah, no! 'twas a butterfly!
Like fragile blossom lying.

Trans. by Clara A. Walsh

Une fleur tombée, à sa branche
Comme je la vois revenir:
C'est un papillon!

Traduit par Michel Revon

[4]

辞　世

朝顔に 今日は見ゆらん 我世かな

守　武

Jisei

Asagao ni
Kyō wa miyuran
Waga yo kana

The Death Verse*

Alas, my lifetime may appear
A morning-glory's hour to-day.

Moritake

The kind of convolvulus often called " morning-glory," much grown in Japan, blooms at dawn and fades at noon; so it becomes a symbol of the briefness of life and life's beauty.

* * * * *

My span of years
To-day appears
A morning-glory's hour.

Trans. by Curtis Hidden Page

Ah ! yes, as a convolvulus
To-day my lifetime will appear.

Trans. by Basil Hall Chamberlain

紹　巴 (姓一里村)
應長五年歿　享年七十九
Shōha (surname, Satomura)
A native of Nara; an instructor
in *renga* (1521–1600)

---

* It was customary for a man of taste, particularly a poet, in Old Japan, to compose a verse on his death-bed, giving expression to his sentiments on his career or on human life.

[5]

梅 の 香

梅の花 香ながらうつす 筆もがな

紹 巴

Ume-no-ka

Ume-no-hana
Ka nagara utsusu
Fude mo gana

The Perfume of Plum-Blossoms

Oh, for a brush which well could paint
The plum-blossoms with their sweet scent!

Shōha

貞 德 (姓一松永)
承應二年歿 享年八十三
Teitoku (surname, Matsunaga) A native of Kyōto; a samurai's son; the founder of the Teitoku School of ***haikai*** (1570–1653)

[6]

秋 の 月

みな人の 晝寢の種や 秋の月

貞 德

Aki-no-Tsuki

Mina hito no
Hirune no tane ya
Aki-no-tsuki

The Autumn Moon

The cause of all men's midday naps—
The autumn moon.

Teitoku

"The autumn moon" or "the moon" means in *haiku* the moon of August fifteenth of the lunar calendar, i.e. of September 22nd or 23rd of the solar calendar, which is in Japan the brightest of all full moons, owing to the particularly transparent atmosphere of this time of the year. This full moon which is the same as the English "harvest moon" is highly appreciated by all people who gaze at it far into the night. The following day, from loss of sleep, they take midday naps. In other words the harvest moon is the *tane* or "seed" i.e. cause of many people's midday naps. Judged by the standard of present day literary *haiku*, this verse, based on reasoning, is mere doggerel. The verses of Teitoku and his disciples are either such pieces, based on reasoning, or pieces whose merit consists in a play on words.

* * * * *

For all men
'Tis the seed of siesta—
The autumn moon.

Trans. by W. G. Aston

'Tis now the season of the Harvest Moon.
Men gaze the livelong night and sow the seed
That brings a sweet siesta on the morrow.

Trans. by Clara A. Walsh

Pour tous les hommes,
Semence du sommeil pendant le jour:
La lune d'automne!

Traduit par Michel Revon

[7]

氷　と　水

打解けて 氷と水の 中なほり

貞　徳

Kōri to Mizu

Uchitokete
Kōri to mizu no
Nakanaori

Ice and Water

Lo, ice and water joyfully
Are reconciled to one another.

Teitoku

The poet means that ice, as spring grows warm, melts into water and joins unfrozen water. In other words, a joyful reconciliation takes place between ice and water. The personification, in which consists the only merit of this verse, is rather witty but can never be considered good taste. This verse belongs to the same grade as " The Autumn Moon."

貞　室（姓一安原）
延寶元年歿　享年六十四
Teishitsu (surname, Yasubara)
A native of Kyōto; Teitoku's pupil (1609–1673)

[8]

吉　野　山　の　櫻

これはこれは とばかり花の 吉野山

貞　室

Yoshino-Yama no Sakura

Korewa korewa
To bakari hana no
Yoshino-yama

The Cherry-Blossoms of Mt. Yoshino

"Oh! Oh!" was all that I could say
On flower-clad Mount Yoshino.

Teishitsu

This is a most famous verse, known to every cultured Japanese. Far more famous are the cherry-blossoms of Mount Yoshino in the province of Yamato. Yoshino is also rich in historic associations. It is there that the Emperor Go-Daigo of the Southern Court resided in exile, so to speak, and died of indignation and despair.

Let it be remembered that "flowers" in ***haiku*** always means "the cherry-blossoms"; and "flower-clad" in this verse means "covered with cherry-blossoms." The poet was overwhelmingly smitten by the beauty of the cherry-blossoms which wrapt the vales and hills of Yoshino, so that he could not but exclaim "Kore-wa! Kore-wa!" or "Oh! Oh!" Some critics say that this verse is not a good piece because this description may be applied to any other beautiful view. For instance, one might as well say:—

"Oh! Oh!" was all that I could say
On peerless snow-capped Mount Fuji.

They are quite right; but I make an exception of this verse which is a spontaneous outburst of profound admiration. I have no hesitation in calling it a beautiful verse.

* * * * *

O this! O this!
Far beyond words it is!
Mountain of cherry bloom, Yoshino-Yama.

Trans. by Curtis Hidden Page

Cherry-blossoms of Yoshino,
These and these only,
Unsurpassed in loveliness,
Yoshino's peerless blossoms!

Trans. by Clara A. Walsh

At lovely Yoshino
The mountain cherries here and there
Have begun to show.

Trans. by William N. Porter

Uttering only
"Oh! Oh! Oh!" I roam over
Yoshino's hills ablow.

Trans. by Inazō Nitobe

"Well well!" and "Well well!"
Is all I can say.—the flowers
On Yoshino mountain!

Trans. by Glenn Shaw

"Oh! Oh!"
All one can say,
Mount Yoshino
In flower gay.

Trans. by Kenzō Wadagaki

Cela, cela
Seulement! En fleurs,
Le mont Yoshino!

Traduit par Michel Revon

[9]

夜 半 の 月

涼しさの かたまりなれや 夜半の月

貞 室

Yowa no Tsuki

Suzushisa no
Katamari nare ya
Yowa no Tsuki

The Bright Moon of Midnight

The bright full moon of midnight—
Perhaps a rounded sphere of coolness.

Teishitsu

Suzushisa or "coolness" is a noun referring to summer; and of course this is the full moon of summer midnight, at sight of which one feels cool and forgets the heat of daytime. The poet likens it to a condensed block of cool, refreshing air.

宗 因 (姓—西山)
天和二年歿 享年七十八
Sō-in (surname, Nishiyama)
A samurai of Kumamoto, later an instructor in *haikai*; the founder of the Danrin School of *haikai* (1604–1682)

[10]

今 宵 の 月

いかないかな 花も今宵の 月一輪

宗 因

Koyoi no Tsuki

Ikana ikana
Hana mo koyoi no
Tsuki ichirin

To-night's Moon

No, no, not even cherry bloom
Can equal the moon of to-night.

Sō-in

"To-night's moon" in ***haiku*** always means the bright full moon of August fifteenth of the lunar calendar, which is the same as the "harvest moon."

[11]

郭　公

郭公　いかに鬼神も　たしかにきけ

宗　因

Hototogisu

Hototogisu
Ikani kijin mo
Tashikani kike

The Cuckoo

The cuckoo is singing;
Ye gods, be sure to listen.

Sō-in

* * * * *

'Tis the cuckoo—
Listen well!
How much soever gods ye be.

Trans. by W. G. Aston

季　吟（姓—北村）
寶永二年歿　享年八十二
Kigin (surname, Kitamura)
A native of Ōmi province; a Shinto priest, later an instructor in poetry (1623–1705)

[12]

名　月

月に寝ぬや　一度にこりず　二度にこりず
季　吟

Meigetsu

Tsuki ni nenu ya
Ichido ni korizu
Nido ni korizu

The Harvest Moon

All night long I watched the glorious moon;
And wearied not the first time nor the second.
Kigin

Meigetsu or "The famous moon" means the harvest moon. The poet enjoyed the bright full moon of August fifteenth of the lunar calendar all night long and watched the moon also the following night, but was not wearied at all. Needless to say this verse is an exaggerated admiration of the beauty of the moonlight. Both the poet and the verse are famous, but it cannot be considered an excellent verse.

* * * * *

All warnings are in vain;
I've suffered once, I've suffered twice,
Yet do the same again.

Trans. by William N. Porter

It is hardly necessary to say that Porter's translation is entirely beside the mark.

[13]

忍　　戀

夏痩と 答へてあとは 涙哉

季　吟

Shinobu Koi

Natsu-yase to
Kotaete ato wa
Namida kana

Unconfessed Love

"Oh, my thinness is caused by summer heat,"
I answered, and burst into tears.

Kigin

The poet imagines himself to be a lovesick young girl who dares not to confess her ardent passion to the man she loves.

The Bashō Period (Approximately, from the middle of the 17th century to the middle of the 18th century, during which Bashō's influence was most predominant)

芭　蕉（姓一松尾）
元祿七年歿　享年五十一
Bashō (surname, Matsuo)
A samurai of Ueno, Iga Province; later an instructor in *haikai*; the founder of the Bashō School of *haikai* (1644–1694)

[14]

元　　日

元日や　思へば淋し　秋の暮

芭　蕉

Gwanjitsu

Gwanjitsu ya
Omoeba sabishi
Aki no kure

New Year's Day

Ah, the New Year's Day reminds me
Of a lonely autumn evening.

Bashō

The poet, who feels happy and joyous on the happiest day in all the year, by and by recalls a past dreary, lonesome autumn evening. Such a mood is quite natural with Bashō, who always enjoyed quietude and lonesomeness.

[15]

雪 の 朝 の 烏

日頃にくき 烏も雪の あしたかな

芭 蕉

Yuki-no-Asa no Karasu

Higoro nikuki
Karasu mo yuki no
Ashita kana

Crows on a Snowy Morning

The usually hateful crow —
How lovely on the morn of snow!

Bashō

It is a snowy morning. As far as eye can reach the world is mantled in virgin snow, which is interspersed here and there with glossy black crows. What a picturesque sight! In this case the crow seems a lovely creature—the unshapely, voracious, harsh-noted, black crow which is usually hateful. The original is of an elegant style, so in the translation "morn" and rhyme are used.

[16]

野 分

猪も 共に吹かるゝ 野分かな

芭 蕉

Nowaki

Inoshishi mo
Tomoni fukaruru
Nowaki kana

The Autumn Tempest

How the autumn storm roars,
Blowing along even wild boars!

Bashō

The tempest is so violent that even strong wild boars are blown along, together with tall grasses and trees. This verse is noted for its graphic description of the power of an autumn storm, and counted one of Bashō's masterpieces.

In Japan violent storms often arise in autumn, and the wind is so powerful that trees in the fields are blown down. Hence the autumn tempest is called *nowaki* or "field-divider."

[17]

高館の廢墟

夏草や　つはものどもが　夢のあと

芭　蕉

Takadachi no Haikyo

Natsugusa ya
Tsuwamono domo ga
Yume no ato

The Ruins of Takadachi Fort

Ah, summer grasses wave!
The warriors' brave deeds were a dream!

Bashō

The original is elliptical and consequently ambiguous, and might lead a casual reader to construe it as:—"Ah! summer grasses wave where the warriors dreamed of glory." The phrase *Yume no ato* which is a puzzel to most readers implies as much as "did heroic deeds which have proved empty as a dream."

The ruins of Takadachi Fort are found at the village of Hiraizume, Iwai County, in the province of Rikuchū. Seven centuries ago General Yoshitsune and his seven or eight loyal men were besieged in this small fort by General Yasuhira's troops. They fought bravely and achieved brilliant deeds, but, far outnumbered, died at last a heroic death.

It is now summer. The ruins are overgrown with grasses. Of old the brave warriors fought against heavy odds and achieved brilliant deeds. But their achievements have proved empty as a dream.

The emotional poet, filled with such reflections, burst into tears, as he confesses in his famous account of travel, "A Narrow Pass through Ōshū."

This is one of Bashō's most famous verses.

* * * * *

Haply the summer grasses are
A relic of the warriors' dream.

Trans. by Basil Hall Chamberlain

Asleep within the grave
The soldiers dream, and overhead
The summer grasses wave.

Trans. by William N. Porter

Old battlefield, fresh with spring flowers again—
All that is left of the dream
Of twice ten thousand warriors slain.

Trans. by Curtis Hidden Page

The summer grass!
'Tis all that's left
Of ancient warriors' dreams.

Trans. by Inazō Nitobe

Ah! les herbes de l'été!
Traces du rêve
Des nombreux guerriers!

Traduit par Michel Revon

[18]

菫　　草

山路來て なにやらゆかし 菫草

芭　蕉

Sumiregusa

Yamaji kite
Naniyara yukashi
Sumiregusa

Violets

Coming along the mountain road I find
Something endearing about violets.

Bashō

The poet alone had trudged for a long while along a mountain road. Quite unexpectedly on a cliff or amidst roadside grasses he espied two or three violets in bloom. Charm-stricken he gazed at the wild flowers for a while with affectionate feelings. *Yukashi* means "attractive" or "endearing" and is different from *okuyukashii* which means "graceful" or "refined."

It is true the Japanese violet possesses no fragrance, but its flowers and leaves have remarkable grace. This verse is worth notice as evincing the poet's love of lowly natural objects.

* * * * *

Beside a mountain path,
A graceful find
Is a tiny violet! Trans. by Minoru Toyoda

Coming this mountain way, no herb
Is lovelier than the violet.
Trans. by Basil Hall Chamberlain

Seek the unperfumed violet
By narrow mountain-pathway set—
Fairest of flowers.

Trans. by Curtis Hidden Page

Chamberlain's mistranslation, "no herb is lovelier than the violet," is due to his misreading *naniyara* or "something" for *naniyori* or "than anything else," which is a serious error. Page's translation is regrettably beside the mark.

[19]

枯枝の烏

枯枝に 烏の止りけり 秋の暮

芭 蕉

Kare-eda no Karasu

Kare eda ni
Karasu no tomari keri
Aki no kure

A Crow on a Bare Branch

A crow is perched on a bare branch;
It is an autumn eve.

Bashō

It is an evening of advanced autumn. A tall tree is standing on the withered moor. Bereft of leaves, its branches are utterly bare. The setting sun shines on the tree-tops and the light is growing faint. A solitary black crow is perched on one of the leafless boughs. What a dreary sight!

The purpose of this verse is an objective portrayal of the dreariness of an autumn evening and its artless art consists in describing a dreary autumn evening without employing the word "dreary." It is an ideal *haiku* of objective portrayal. The word *kare-eda* has two meanings:—a dead branch or a leafless branch. Here it means "a leafless branch." *Aki-no-kure* means "an autumn evening," not "late autumn" for which *haijin* have the phrase *kure-no-aki*. The number of *karasu* is not definitely expressed, therefore the uninitiated might construe it "some crows." But it is hardly necessary to say that Bashō means "a solitary crow," otherwise his intention of portraying a dreary autumn evening could not be attained. A picture by the poet himself of this verse proves this conclusively.

One of the two translations of this verse in the first edition of the present volume :—

> Lo! a crow sits on a bare bough;
> 'Tis a *dreary* autumn evening.

is clumsy because it contains "dreary," a superfluous word. The second line of the original has nine syllables instead of the regular seven. Bashō sometimes resorted to redundant syllables for the sake of the sense.

This verse was composed in the autumn of 1680, when Bashō was thirty-seven years old. It is one of his most famous verses and generally considered one of his masterpieces. Until about 1678 Bashō had been a poet of the Danrin School whose style is characterized by puns on words and low wit, but he was now a poet in the true sense of the term. It may safely be said that his characteristic style—a serious, quiet, refined, naturalistic and at the same time, strange to say, subjective style—dates from this verse on "A Crow on A Bare Branch." This is an epoch-making verse which took the first step in the movement elevating the *haikai* to serious, pure literature.

* * * * *

> The end of autumn, and some rooks
> Are perched upon a withered branch.
>
> Trans. by Basil Hall Chamberlain

> The autumn gloaming deepens into night;
> Black 'gainst the slowly-fading orange light,
> On withered bough a lonely crow is sitting.
>
> Trans. by Clara A. Walsh

On a withered branch
A crow is sitting
This autumn eve. Trans. by W. G. Aston

[20]

古　池

古池や 蛙飛びこむ 水の音

芭　蕉

Furuike

Furuike ya
Kawazu tobikomu
Mizu no oto

The Old Pond

(A)
The ancient pond!
A frog plunged—splash!

(B)
The old pond! A frog plunged—
The sound of the water!

Bashō

This verse is far more famous than "A Crow on A Bare Branch," and it is no exaggeration to say there is not a Japanese but knows it by heart. It was composed in March, 1685, that is, five years later than "A Crow on A Bare Branch." What importance Bashō attached to it may well be inferred from the following fact. Asked by some of his disciples for a death-verse in his dying moments, the poet is said to have answered:—"Every verse I have composed since I originated my own style typified by

The ancient pond!
A frog plunged—splash!

—every verse composed by myself since then is my death-verse......" Naturally enough his disciples regarded this verse with a reverence verging on superstition. It teems with fables, traditions and far-fetched theories, and commentators go so far as to call it a moral and religious lesson expounding a doctrine of Buddhism. On the other hand, as a reactionary tendency, modern iconoclasts consider it as a commonplace verse below notice. In my opinion both views are wrong. It is true that this verse is not Bashō's greatest masterpiece; but nobody could reasonably object to calling it a representative verse which occupies a highly important position in the history of *haikai*. It was indeed by "A Crow on A Bare Branch" and more emphatically by the present verse that Bashō, quite discontented with the verses of his predecessors and his contemporaries, which were all comic and too artifical, clumsy and shallow, endeavoured to show model verses which aim at mysticism, quietude and naturalism. In this verse was found an indisputable criterion for literary *haiku*, which has continued up to the present day to exert a boundless influence on *haijin*.

Close to Bashō's hut there was a small fish-pond which had been long in disuse and in which, it is probable, many frogs dwelt. One quiet spring afternoon, while Bashō was buried in thought, he heard a faint noise which suddenly broke the deathlike stillness. It was a splash!—the sound of a frog leaping into the water! Then Bashō felt that the almost melancholy quietude of the spring day had been intensified. That moment the following lines escaped his lips:—

Kawazu tobikomu
Mizu no oto

or "A frog plunged —
The sound of the water."

"Well......let me see......" the poet thought to himself. "These words are quite sufficient for expressing my feelings of this moment. But as a *haiku* they are insufficient. The first five syllables are lacking. Then what words shall I add?" Bashō was puzzled. Just at this moment his disciple Kikaku called. Bashō put this problem to him. After a few moments' reflection the younger poet proposed:—

Yamabuki ya

or "The globe-flowers!"

Probably this phrase referred to some globe-flowers which were in bloom by the fish-pond. But Bashō would not accept it. He thought "The globe-flowers!" was rather too gay. He wanted a sober, plain phrase which would suit those two lines. After short search, Bashō hit upon *Furuike ya*! or "The ancient pond!" a phrase perfectly in keeping with the calm atmosphere of

"A frog plunged—
The sound of the water!"

It is worth while to notice that this verse is one which appeals to the ear, not to the eye.

* * * * *

Into an old pond
A frog took a sudden plunge,
Then is heard a splash.

Trans. by Inazō Nitobe

Old garden lake!
The frog thy depth doth seek,
And sleeping echoes wake.

Trans. by Hidesaburō Saitō

An ancient pond!
A frog leaps in;
The sound of the water!

Trans. by Minoru Toyoda

The old pond, aye! and the sound of a frog leaping into the water.

Trans. by Basil Hall Chamberlain

A lonely pond in age-old stillness sleeps......
Apart, untirred by sound or motion......till
Suddenly into it a lithe frog leaps.

Trans. by Curtis Hidden Page

An old-time pond, from off whose shadowed depth
Is heard the splash where some lithe frog leaps in.

Trans. by Clara A. Walsh

The old pond!
A frog leapt into—
List, the water sound!

Trans. by Yone Noguchi

Into the calm old lake
A frog with flying leap goes plop!
The peaceful hush to break.

Trans. by William N. Porter

An ancient pond!
With a sound from the water
Of the frog as it plunges in.

Trans. by W. G. Aston

Ah! le vieil étang!
Et le bruit de l'eau
Où saute la grenouille!

Traduit par Michel Revon

[21]

今　日　の　月

三井寺の 門たゝかばや 今日の月

芭　蕉

Kyō-no-Tsuki

Miidera no
Kado tatakaba ya
Kyō-no-tsuki

To-night's Moon

Ah! to knock at Mii Temple's gate,
And there behold to-night's full moon!

Bashō

Kyō-no-tsuki or "to-day's moon" i.e. "to-night's full moon" means the harvest moon. The Buddhist temple of Miidera, one of the most famous temples, stands on a hill commanding an entrancing view of Lake Biwa. On that particular night Bashō, with some friends, was contemplating the moonlight at the Gichūji Temple situated at a little distance on the shore of the lake; and he was so bewitched by the beautiful sight that he was much inclined to call at the Miidera Temple for further enjoyment of the moon. In this seemingly worthless verse, Bashō resorts to the indirect method of admiring the beautiful moonlight by simply mentioning that he would fain call at the Miidera Temple, which is rich in historical associations and celebrated for beautiful views.

* * * * *

Of Miidera
The gate I would knock at—
The moon of to-day.

Trans. by W. G. Aston

[22]

蟬（無常迅速）

やがて死ぬ けしきは見えず 蟬の聲

芭　蕉

Semi (*Mujō Jinsoku*)

Yagate shinu
Keshiki wa miezu
Semi no koe

Cicadas (Fleeting Life)

There is no sign in the cicadas' cry
That they are just about to die.

Bashō

It is the hot midday of summer. All round cicadas are deafeningly crying *jii-jii-jii* . . . Their lusty cries do not give the slightest intimation that they are fated presently to die. All living things, human beings included of course, share the same melancholy lot! Ah! how fleeting life is! This verse may well be considered a Buddhist sermon, preaching that human life is transient like the morning dew or lightning flashes. In this respect it is disparagingly spoken of by some modern critics, although it is generally considered one of Bashō's best verses.

* * * * *

Never an intimation in all those voices of *semi*......how quickly the hush will come,......how speedily all must die.

Trans. by Lafcadio Hearn

O cricket, from your cherry cry
No one could ever guess
How quickly you must die.

Trans. by Curtis Hidden Page

The cry of the cicada
Gives no sign,
That presently it will die.

Trans. by W. G. Aston

Qu'elle doit bientôt mourir,
A son aspect il ne parait pas,
La voix de la cigale!

Traduit par Michel Revon

[23]

月 と 梅

春もやゝ けしきとゝのふ 月と梅

芭 蕉

Tsuki to Ume

Haru mo yaya
Keshiki tōtonō
Tsuki to ume

The Moon and The Plum-Blossoms

The spring scene is wellnigh prepared—
The hazy moon and plum-blossoms.

Bashō

The New Year has come, and spring has set in; the pure, fragrant and hardy plum-blossoms, the forerunners of spring flowers, have just bloomed, and the hazy spring moon is shining on their snow-white petals. This picturesque sight is a favourite subject for Oriental artists. This verse, which well depicts the characteristics of early spring, is indeed worthy of the greatest of ***haijin.***

[24]

桐葉のもとを別るゝとて

牡丹蘂 深く分出る蜂の 名殘かな

芭 蕉

Tōyō no Moto wo Wakaruru Tote

Botan-shibe
Fukaku wake-izuru hachi no
Nagori kana

At Parting With Tōyō

How reluctantly the bee emerges from
The depths of pistils of a peony!

Bashō

This is a farewell verse composed by Bashō at taking leave of Tōyō, a pupil in Owari Province, at whose residence the poet has stayed for a long while. The peony in question may well be imagined to be an exceedingly beautiful large-petaled one. A bee, which dived deep among its pistils and sucked the nectar to its heart's content, has now reluctantly emerged. Needless to say, the bee is Bashō himself who has been treated with great hospitality at his pupil's house and has felt himself quite at home. It is with great reluctance that he is now parting with his kind friend. The translator highly appreciates the beautiful metaphor. It is noteworthy that the second line consists of eleven syllables instead of the regular seven—the longest redundant line in Bashō's ***haiku***—yet it does not spoil the rhythm of the whole verse.

[25]

馬　上　吟

道のべの 木槿は馬に 喰はれけり

芭　蕉

Bajō Gin

Michi-no-be no
Mukuge wa uma ni
Kuware keri

A Verse Composed on Horseback

A roadside althæa
Was eaten by my horse.

Bashō

The *mukuge, mokuge,* or *hachisu* is the hibiscus, a kind of althæa. It is an ornamental shrub with white, red, purple or blue flowers which bloom in the morning and fade in the evening. It is cultivated generally for a hedge. In 1684, three years after the appearance of his verse, "A Crow on a Bare Branch," he made a pilgrimage along the Tōkaidō. One day the footsore poet hired a horse; and while he was waiting on horseback for his attendant to walk up to him, his horse bit off a branch of an althæa in the hedge of a farmer's house, and devoured it in a moment. Then the above verse escaped his lips. "He wondered," Seisensui says in 'Bashō the Traveller,' "whether this artless description of a trivial occurrence might be a verse. After a moment's reflection he thought, 'A commonplace occurrence, described as it is, is precious. It is wrong to resort to tricks in composing *haiku.* Looking at nature as it is and portraying nature as it is—this should be a *haijin's* attitude.'" Seisensui's judgment hits the mark, and it is an overstrained interpretation—perpetrated by some commentators of old—to construe this verse as a demonstration of the moral lesson that the vulgar yearning for fame and distinction can lead only to misery. "This verse is a realistic description of an incident on a journey," says Meisetsu, "and a charming sketch of a country scene."

* * * * *

The mallow-flower by the road
Was eaten by a (passing) horse.

Trans. by Basil Hall Chamberlain

The roadside thistle, eager
To see the travellers pass
Was eaten by the passing ass.

Trans. by William N. Porter

Au bord du chemin
La guimauve en arbre, par le cheval
A été mangée......

Traduit par Michel Revon

[26]

雪（去年のわび寝をおもひ出て越人に贈る）

二人見し 雪は今年も 降りけるか

芭　蕉

Yuki ***(Kozo no wabine wo omoi-idete Etsujin ni okuru)***

Futari mishi
Yuki wa kotoshi mo
Furikeru ka

Snow

(Sent to Etsujin at the recollection of last year's journey)

The snow we two beheld —
Hath it come down again this year?

Bashō

The season of snow had come round again. Bashō recalled the cold yet beautiful snowfall that he and Etsujin, his favourite pupil, had experienced in the previous winter in Owari, the province of the latter. A simple, artless verse, alive with a longing for travel and affectionate feelings toward a pupil—symbolic of the poet's character.

[27]

天　の　川

荒海や 佐渡によこたふ 天の川

芭　蕉

Ama-no-gawa

Ara-umi ya
Sado ni yokotō
Ama-no-gawa

The Milky Way

The sea is wild! The Milky Way extends
Far over to the island of Sado.

Bashō

This is a night view Bashō enjoyed at Izumozaki, a seaport in Echigo Province. The Japan Sea is high with billows; and the Milky Way streams overhead across to the island of Sado, some sixty miles off, which looks clear and beautiful in the starlight.

This verse is universally considered a masterpiece which exhibits, in the insignificant compass of seventeen syllables, a magnificent scene combining a firmament glittering with the Milky Way (called in Japanese *Ama-no-gawa* or Heaven's River), an expanse of high seas and a distant solitary island.

* * * * *

A rough sea, and the Milky Way
Stretching across to Sado's isle.

Trans. by Basil Hall Chamberlain

The sea is rough;
Over the island of Sado
Extends the Milky Way.

Trans. by Minoru Toyoda

O rough sea! Waves on waves do darkling rise,
The galaxy reaching down where Sado lies.

Trans. by Shigeru Nishimura

The billows come rolling,
And the Milky Way
Stretches across to the Sado Islands.

Trans. by S. H. Wainright

[28]

晝 の 螢

晝見れば 首筋赤き 螢かな

芭 蕉

Hiru no Hotaru

Hiru mireba
Kubisuji Akaki
Hotaru kana

The Firefly Seen by Daylight

Alas! the firefly seen by daylight
Is nothing but a red-necked insect.

Bashō

A typical example of disillusionment.

* * * * *

Oh, this firefly!—seen by daylight, the nape of its neck is red!

Trans. by Lafcadio Hearn

[29]

最 上 川

五月雨を 集めて早し 最上川

芭 蕉

Mogami-gawa

Samidare wo
Atsumete hayashi
Mogami-gawa

The Mogami River

Collecting all the rains of May,
How swiftly flows the Mogami!

Bashō

Samidare or "The May rains" are the rains which continue some three weeks in May of the lunar calendar. The Mogami-gawa, which flows through the northeast of Uzen Province, is considered one of the three most rapid streams in Japan. In the rainy season it rises high and runs swiftly as an arrow.

Here we find a vivid description of a great river flowing in torrents. The figure, "Collecting all the rains of May," is incomparable.

* * * * *

How swiftly move
The June rains,
Brought together,
In the Mogami River!

Trans. by S. H. Wainright

With all the waters of the season's rain
The Mogami doth rush into the main.

Trans. by S. Nishimura

[30]

古 寺 翫 月

月見する 座に美しき 顔もなし

芭 蕉

Koji Gwangetsu

Tsukimi suru
Za ni utsukushiki
Kawo mo nashi

Moon Viewing at an Old Temple

No pretty face is to be seen
Among the group viewing the moon.

Bashō

"The moon" in *haiku* signifies the harvest moon. The chief merit of this impromptu verse, composed at a moon-viewing party, consists in eulogizing the beauty of the moon without employing a single word in its praise.

[31]

奈良に出る道のほど

春なれや 名もなき山の 朝霞

芭 蕉

Nara ni Izuru Michi no Hodo

Haru nareya
Na mo naki yama no
Asa-gasumi

On the Way to Nara

Thanks to Spring, a nameless hill
Has its veil of morning mist.

Bashō

It is indeed owing to Spring that even a commonplace hill, which is usually noticed by nobody, looks picturesque, covered with a beautiful veil of morning haze.

A simple, yet beautiful sketch of a spring height. The quiet rhythm and sweet melody of the original are noteworthy.

[32]

船　頭

春風や 烟管啣へて 船頭殿

芭　蕉

Sendō

Harukaze ya
Kiseru kuwaete
Sendo-dono

The Boatman

Lo! in the spring breeze, pipe in mouth,
Mr. Boatman waits for passengers.

Bashō

An interesting sketch of a ferry on a balmy spring day. Notice the humour in the title of "Mr. Boatman."

Although it may not be called a masterpiece, this verse possesses humour and some dignity, and is quite worthy of Bashō. Literally translated, the original is as follows:—

"A spring breeze!
Pipe in mouth,
Mr. Ferryman......"

[33]

草　　庵

蓑蟲の 音をきゝに來よ 草の庵

芭　蕉

Sōan

Minomushi no
Ne wo kikini koyo
Kusa no io

My Cottage

O, friend, come to my hut
To hear the bagworms' voice.

Bashō

This verse is said to have been sent to Ransetsu, Bashō's favourite pupil. Tradition says that the bagworm chirps in a feeble, sad voice, longing for its parents, and has been a favourite insect with poets from of old. I cannot but feel that this verse symbolizes Bashō's life of quietude. 庵 is pronounced either "iori" or simply "io."

* * * * *

Come to listen
To the basket-worms,
To my lowly hut.

Trans. by Minoru Toyoda

[34]

子 規 と 月

子規 大竹藪を もる月夜

芭 蕉

Hototogisu to Tsuki

Hototogisu
Ō-takeyabu wo
Moru tsukiyo

A Cuckoo and the Moon

A cuckoo has cried; lo! the moon
Gleams through a great grove of bamboos.

Bashō

This verse was composed at the village of Saga, near Kyōto, which abounds in bamboo groves.

It is a summer night. A cuckoo, crying shrilly, has flown across the sky. Behold! in the same direction there is a great grove of bamboos looming black. A closer observation reveals pale moonbeams glittering through the grove. What a weird and mystic scene!

Let it be remembered that, unlike the English bird, the Japanese cuckoo is shrill and often flies and calls at dawn.

[35]

鶉

鷹の目も いまや暮ぬと 啼鶉

芭 蕉

Uzura

Taka no me mo
Ima ya kure nu to
Naku uzura

The Quails

The quails are chirping in the dusk
Aware the hawks' eyes are now dim.

Bashō

Needless to say this is a manifestation of the poet's deep svmpathy for weaker birds.

[36]

初　雪

初雪や 水仙の葉の たはむまで

芭　蕉

Hatsuyuki

Hatsuyuki ya
Suisen no ha no
Tawamu made

The First Snow

The first snow—just enough
To bend the jonquil leaves.

Bashō

The first snow has fallen, just enough to bend the leaves of the frail jonquils —a natural and yet skilful method of suggesting that the snowfall is not heavy.

[37]

萩　と　月

一家に 遊女も寐たり 萩と月

芭　蕉

Hagi to Tsuki

Hitotsu-ya ni
Yūjo mo netari
Hagi to tsuki

Lespedeza Flowers and the Moon

Courtezans and I lodged in the same inn —
Lespedeza flowers and the bright moon.

Bashō

Most scholars pronounce "一家" *Hitotsu-ya*; but Seisensui asserts that it ought to be pronounced *hitotsu-ie* which means "the same house," not *hitotsuya,* which means "a solitary house."

「寐たり」 or *netari* literally translated, means "slept" but here "lodged" is more appropriate.

This verse appears in Bashō's famous account of travel, *Oku no Hosomichi* or "A Narrow Pass Through Ōshū." During his weary journey, the poet happened one night to put up with two courtezans, at the same inn in the village of Ichifuri, in the province of Echigo. As he overheard, through paper partitions, their conversation with a man companion, Bashō was fascinated by a beautiful scene in the garden—pretty lespedeza flowers bathed in the bright moonlight. The following morning the frail ladies humbly asked him to be their companion and protector on their pilgrimage to the sacred Ise Temples, but he reluctantly and politely refused their request. On this occasion, out of compassion for these girls, he burst into the above verse. It is undeniable that the flowers are likened to the girls and the moon to himself. This is the only one among Bashō's numerous verses that has for its theme a rather romantic incident, suitable for a short story. Personally I appreciate it; but it is the opinion of some commentators that this verse, which deals with such complicated feelings, is open to critism.

[38]

稲 妻 (或知識のたまはく なま禪大疵のもとゐとかや、いと有がたく覺えて。)

稲妻に さとらぬ人の 貴さよ

芭 蕉

Inazuma

Inazuma ni
Satoranu hito no
Tōtosa yo

Lightning

(In high appreciation of the remark of a Buddhist priest of profound wisdom, "A smattering of the Zen cult is at the bottom of grave errors.")

How noble he who realizes not,
From lightning-flashes, life is vain!

Bashō

This verse, needless to say, reproves a superficial realization of the vanity of life and a pessimist who says "Life is fleeting as lightning! Life is but an empty dream!" Most critics do not set a high value on such didactic ***haiku*** as this.

[**39**]

最　上　川

あつき日を　海に入れたり　最上川

芭　蕉

Mogami-gawa

Atsuki hi wo
Umi ni iretari
Mogami-gawa

The Mogami River

Behold! the Mogami has sunk
The burning sun into the sea.

Bashō

The hot summer sun is now sinking into the Japan Sea, just opposite the spot where the mighty Mogami river is rushing into the main; and a refreshing, cool evening is steadily approaching. Bashō who was struck by this magnificent scene, probably on Mount Hiyoriyama at Sakata, the estuary port, figuratively says, "The Mogami river has sunk the hot sun into the sea." Therein consists the poet's techinique of no common measure.

* * * * *

The Mogami river
Has washed the hot sunshine
Down into the sea.

Trans. by S. H. Wainright

[40]

鵜　　船

おもしろうて やがて悲しき 鵜船かな

芭　蕉

Ubune

Omoshirōte
Yagate kanashiki
Ubune kana

The Cormorant Fishing Boat

I felt gay, but presently sad,
In the cormorant fishing boat.

Bashō

This was composed when Bashō saw cormorant fishing on the Nagara-gawa, in the province of Mino. It is an extremely curious method of fishing *ayu*, a kind of fresh-water trout, by the help of cormorants elaborately trained for the purpose. Each cormorant wears at the base of its neck a whalebone ring drawn tight enough to prevent marketable fish from passing below it. Each fisherman deftly manipulates a dozen cormorants by cords attached to them. A magnificent sight is presented, in the darkness of moonless night, by several boats with fishermen skilfully handling tens of cormorants which dive bravely in the water bathed in bright torch-light. Bashō, who witnessed the spectacle for the first time, felt great delight. But presently the fishermen lifted the birds aboard, forced their bills open and squeezed their swollen necks, when living silvery fish were vomited. The commpassionate poet could not but feel melancholy at the sight of this cunning artifice, plundering what the birds had caught with great labour.

* * * * *

D'abord joyeux
Et bientôt triste,
Le bateau de cormorans!

Traduit par Michel Revon

[41]

野明亭にて

すゞしさを 繪にうつし鳬 嵯峨の竹

芭蕉

Yamei-tei Nite

Suzushisa wo
E ni utsushi-keri
Saga no take

At Yamei's House

How cool are these Saga bamboos! —
A picture of refreshing air.

Bashō

As stated above under the verse (34), "A Cuckoo and the Moon," Saga, near Kyōto, abounds in bamboo groves. This verse means;—"How cool and refreshing these bamboo groves are! They are, so to speak, a picture representing refreshing air." It was composed when Bashō stayed at the house of his pupil Yamei, a native of Saga. It was a compliment to his host.

[42]

藤の花

草臥れて 宿かるころや 藤の花

芭蕉

Fuji-no-Hana

Kutabire-te
Yado karu koro ya
Fuji-no-hana

Wistaria Flowers

I came weary, seeking an inn —
When lo, these wistaria flowers!

Bashō

One evening during his pilgrimage in the province of Yamato, Bashō was about to seek an inn at the town of Tamba-ichi. Just at this moment some lovely wistaria flowers blooming by the wayside caught his eye. Spellbound by their beauty, the poet paused for a while, quite unconscious of his fatigue.

* * * * *

I come aweary,
In search of an inn—
Ah! these wistaria flowers!

Trans. by W. G. Aston

Tired with travelling
I think of a lodging;
Ah! the drooping wistaria!

Trans. by Minoru Toyoda

[43]

和二角蓼螢句一

あさがほに 我は食くふ をとこ哉

芭　蕉

Kaku no Tade to Hotaru no Ku ni Wasu

Asagao ni
Ware wa meshi kuu
Otoko kana

In Imitation of Kaku's Haiku on Knotgrass and a Firefly

Ah! I take my breakfast,
Viewing morning glories.

Bashō

A more exact translation is as follows:—

Ah! I am a man breakfasting
In the presence of morning glories.

This verse was composed in imitation of the phraseology of his favourite pupil Kikaku's conceited *haiku*:—

草の戸に 我は蓼くふ 螢哉

Kusa no to ni
Ware wa tade kuu
Hotaru kana

Ah! I am a firefly eating
Knotgrass in a thatched hut.

Bashō sent it to Kikaku, tradition says, as a warning against his intemperance in eating and drinking. Whatever be the case, it treats of his austerely beauty-loving life. In contradistinction to his pupil's sumptuous and rather indolent style of living, Bashō rose early and took his simple breakfast, gazing at pure and lovely morning glories blooming in his garden.

[44]

夏　野

馬ほくほく　われを繪に見る　夏野哉

芭　蕉

Natsu-No

Uma hokuhoku
Ware wo e ni miru
Natsu-no kana

The Summer Moor

My horse ambles clop-clop across the summer moor;
I find myself in a picture.

Bashō

Imagine Bashō in priestly garb on horseback. It is a warm, breezy day in early summer. His horse goes along at an easy pace over a verdant moor; and the poet feels himself to be in a beautiful picture.

A melodious verse precisely in keeping with the poet's mood.

[45]

閑な住居

木啄の　柱をたゝく　住居かな

芭　蕉

Shizukana Sumai

Kitsutsuki no
Hashira wo tataku
Sumai kana

A Quiet Abode

What a quiet abode!
A woodpecker pecks at its posts.

Bashō

An exaggerated description of a quiet hut.

[**46**]

菜　　蟲

胡蝶にも　ならで秋ふる　菜蟲哉

芭　蕉

Namushi

Kochō nimo
Narade aki furu
Namushi kana

The Rape-Worm

Alas! the rape-worms writhe in autumn wind
Without e'en turning into butterflies.

Bashō

What a pitiable worm! Unlike most caterpillars, the rape-worm does not turn into a beautiful butterfly, but always remains a hateful, ugly worm until it dies in autumn.

A pathetic verse hinting at the fate of most men.

[47]

虻 （物皆自得）

花を吸ふ 虻なくらひそ 友すゞめ

芭 蕉

Abu (***Mono Mina Jitoku Su***)

Hana wo suu
Abu na kuraiso
Tomo-suzume

The Horse-Fly (**Everything has its Place.**)

Friend sparrows, don't eat those horse-flies,
Which suck the nectar of flowers.

Bashō

A didactic verse implying that all creatures have their place in nature and threfore should not try to destory one another.

* * * * *

Moineau, mon ami!
Ne mange pas l'abeille
Qui se joue sur les fleurs!

Traduit par Michel Revon

[48]

春 の 夜

春の夜は 櫻に明けて 仕舞ひけり

芭 蕉

Haru-no-Yo

Haru-no-yo wa
Sakura ni akete
Shimai keri

The Spring Night

Alas! the sweet spring night has gone
While we the cherry-flowers viewed.

Bashō

The Japanese often enjoy a night scene of cherry-blossoms illuminated with gay paper lanterns.

* * * * *

Feasting beneath the cherry-flowers gay,
Heedlesss of the swift fleeting hours, we stay,
Until the vernal night has passed away.

Trans. by Kenzō Wadagaki

La nuit de printemps:
Les cerisiers! Aux cerisiers
L'aurore est venue!

Traduit par Michel Revon

[49]

花 の 蔭

花の蔭 謠に似たる 旅寝かな

芭 蕉

Hana no Kage

Hana no gage
Utai ni nitaru
Tabine kana

Under Cherry-Blossoms

While touring I slept under cherry-bloom;
Which calls to mind the scene of a *Nō* play.

Bashō

This verse was composed when Bashō stayed overnight at the village of Kusao in Yamato Province. Probably in the garden of the inn, cherry-trees were in full bloom, whose sight he enjoyed far into the night, thinking with delight perhaps of the *Nō* play, "Tadanori," the theme of which is the protagonist's famous poem:—

ゆきくれて 木の下かげを 宿とせば
花やこよひの あるじならまし

Yuki-kurete
Kono-shita kage wo
Yado to seba
Hana ya koyoi no
Aruji naramashi

By darkness overta'en and spent,
To me a cherry-tree its shelter lent;
As hosts and friends its blossoms fair
To-night will solace all my care.

If my interpretation is right, "I slept under cherry-bloom" is figurative language. The original is quite rhythmical although it cannot be called a masterpiece.

[50]

雉子の聲

蛇くふと 聞けばおそろし 雉子の聲

芭蕉

Kiji no Koe

Hebi kuu to
Kikeba osoroshi
Kiji no koe

The Pheasant's Voice

Having heard it devours the snake,
How horrid sounds the pheasant's voice!

Bashō

An interesting contrast between the beautiful bird and its ugly act.

This verse suggests to Japanese readers the saying 外面如菩薩內心如夜叉 *Gemen nyo bosatsu naishin nyo yasha* or "An angel in countenance, a devil at heart."

* * * * *

Qu'il mange les serpents,
En apprenant cela, combien terrible
La voix du faisan vert!

Traduit par Michel Revon

[51]

雲　　雀

雲雀より 上に休らふ 峠かな

芭　蕉

Hibari

Hibari yori
Ue ni yasurō
Tōge kana

The Lark

We took rest on a mountain pass
Even above the soaring lark.

Bashō

The mountain pass on which the poet took rest was so high that the voice of a soaring skylark was audible below him. This witty observation is the chief merit of the verse.

[52]

鶯

鶯や 柳のうしろ 藪の前

芭　蕉

Uguisu

Uguisu ya
Yanagi no ushiro
Yabu no mae

Nightingales

The nightingales are singing sweet
Behind willows, before the grove.

Bashō

A beautiful verse portraying a balmy spring day in the country.

The *uguisu* or "Japanese nightingale" is a little larger than the European nightingale and sings in the daytime. It is the sweetest of Japanese songsters.

[53]

梅　の　花

忘るなよ　藪の中なる　梅の花

芭　蕉

Ume-no-Hana

Wasuruna yo
Yabu no naka naru
Ume no hana

The Plum-Blossoms

Pray, don't forget, my friend,
The plum-bloom in the grove.

Bashō

This is a farewell verse given to a pupil starting on a journey in Michi-no-ku. Michi-no-ku is the ancient general name for the present provinces of Iwaki, Iwashiro, Rikuzen, Rikuchū, and Mutsu. Needless to say, Bashō likens himself to the plum-blossoms blushing unseen in the thicket.

[54]

日 の 出

梅が香に のつと日の出る 山路かな

芭 蕉

Hi-no-De

Ume-ga-ka ni
Notto hi no deru
Yamaji kana

The Sunrise

On the mountain road the sun arose
Suddenly in the fragrance of plum-flowers.

Bashō

This is generally counted among Bashō's best verses. It is really a supreme masterpiece of realistic description.

When the poet, an early riser, had climbed a mountain road, day had dawned. At this moment he perceived a sweet fragrance. Looking about he descried white plum-blossoms all round in the vales and on the slopes. While he paused, bewitched by the scenery, the great ball of the red sun rose suddenly, shedding its radiance on the snow-white petals. A very beautiful scene!

[55]

郭 公

郭公 啼き啼き飛ぶぞ いそがはし

芭 蕉

Hototogisu

Hototogisu
Naki-naki tobu zo
Isogawashi

The Cuckoo

The cuckoo leads a busy life,
Ever calling as it flies.

Bashō

[56]

瀬 田 の 橋

五月雨に かくれぬものや 瀬田の橋

芭　蕉

Seta-no-Hashi

Samidare ni
Kakurenu mono ya
Seta-no-hashi

Seta Bridge

'Tis only Seta Bridge which is
Unhidden in the rains of May.

Bashō

The " Long Bridge of Seta " spans the waters of Lake Biwa at the picturesque spot where it narrows to form the Seta-gawa.

The rains of May (the modern June) have continued for several days, so that the lake and the hills around it are veiled in the downpour. But the "Long Bridge of Seta" alone looms visible like a rainbow.

[57]

長良川十八樓

此のあたり 目に見ゆるもの 皆涼し

芭 蕉

Nagara-gawa Jūhachi-Rō

Kono atari
Me ni miyuru mono
Mina suzushi

The Jūhachi-Rō on the Nagara River

Here everything is cool
Which comes within my sight.

Bashō

The Jūhachi-Rō or "The Home of Eighteen Views" was the house of Kajima, Bashō's pupil, built on the Nagara-gawa, in the province of Mino. Bashō named it so, because, in his opinion, the fresh, cool air enjoyed at the house was worth "the Eight Views on the Siao and the Siang" and "the Ten Views of Lake Si" in China; and this verse was composed in eulogy of it.

[58]

夏 野

秣負ふ 人を枝折の 夏野かな

芭 蕉

Natsuno

Magusa ou
Hito wo shiori no
Natsuno kana

The Summer Moor

Our guide—unconscious guide—across the summer moor—
A man carrying horse-fodder on his Back.
Bashō

Bashō, accompanied by his pupil Sora, was trudging over the Nasuno Plain, which was a vast wilderness in his day. They were in danger of losing their way; but, luckily enough, they descried ahead, at no great distance, a farmer with fodder for his horse on his back. Unseen they followed him, making an unconscious guide of him, so to speak. A beautiful sketch of a summer moor.

[59]

栗 の 花

世の人の 見付けぬ花や 軒の栗
芭 蕉

Kuri-no-Hana

Yono hito no
Mitsukenu hana ya
Noki no kuri

The Chestnut Flowers

Quite unknown to the passers-by —
The chestnut-flowers by your house.

Bashō

One day during his journey through Ōshū, Bashō called on a Buddhist priest named Kashin who lived a life of seclusion. His cottage stood under a great sweet chestnut-tree which was just in bloom. The chestnut flowers were so plain that they were unnoticed by passers-by. It was true, Bashō thought, they bloomed and faded, unseen by men, but they could enjoy an easy and secure life. The poet likens the chestnut-flowers to the priest who led a pure and unpretentious life, far from the madding crowd.

[60]

栗 の 毬

秋風の 吹けども青し 栗のいが

芭 蕉

Kuri no Iga

Akikaze no
Fukedomo aoshi
Kuri no iga

The Chestnut Burs

Although the autumn wind blows now,
The chestnut burs are green.

Bashō

The autumn wind is blowing. Almost all green plants have turned yellow and are withering; but the chestnut burs undauntedly resist the blighting wind and remain fresh and green. Their hardiness strikes the poet's admiration and the verse implies nothing else. Some commentators think quite otherwise, saying that Bashō likens his own frailty to the chestnut bur which remains green when other things grow mellow in autumn.

[61]

落　葉

留守の間に　あれたる神の　落葉かな

芭　蕉

Ochiba

Rusu no mani
Aretaru kami no
Ochiba kana

Fallen Leaves

In his absence the god's garden
Is neglected, dead leaves piling.

Bashō

A realistic description of the garden of the Gongen Shrine at Numazu in the province of Suruga. In October of the lunar calendar, tradition says, the gods and goddesses of all the shrines throughout the Empire visit the Great Izumo Shrine to attend a sacred conclave. Therefore October is called *Kami-na-zuki* or "the God-less Month." When Bashō visited the Gongen Shrine in October, the garden was found entirely neglected, fallen leaves piled up all round, because the god was away in Izumo. A somewhat humorous verse.

[62]

雪　の　朝

馬をさへ ながむる雪の あしたかな

芭　蕉

Yuki no Asa

Uma wo sae
Nagamuru yuki no
Ashita kana

The Snowy Morning

Ah! on the snowy morning,
We gaze even at horses.

Bashō

Usually we take no notice of passing horses; but on a snowy morning, even horses look particularly beautiful and attract our attention. In other words, all things look beautiful in snow. *Ashita* in literary language means "morning," though in popular language "to-morrow."

[63]

雀

菜畠に 花見顔なる 雀哉

芭　蕉

Suzume

Nabatake ni
Hanami-gao naru
Suzume kana

Sparrows

In the rape field, the sparrows look
As if they are viewing the flowers.

Bashō

This verse was composed probably in the province of Ōmi. Even at the present day around Lake Biwa there are to be seen numerous fields of rape; and a little past mid-spring, a vast expanse of golden rape-flowers, interspersed with silvery radish-flowers, presents an exceedingly beautiful sight, together with their reflections in the still waters of the lake. In such a field of rape-flowers, some sparrows are found, looking as if they are gazing at the beautiful flowers. *Hanami-gao*, literally translated, means "flower-viewing faces."

[64]

伊勢の大廟に詣でゝ

何の木の 花とはしらず 匂ひ哉

芭　蕉

Ise-no-Taibyō ni Mōdete

Nan no ki no
Hana towa shirazu
Nioi kana

Worshipping at the Great Ise Shrines

I cannot tell what flowers it came from,
But an unnameable fragrance filled me.

Bashō

While worshipping at the Great Ise Shrines, the most sacred of all Japanese shrines, Bashō was overwhelmingly struck with the divine power; and he likens the indescribable feelings he experienced to the perception of a powerful fragrance from some unknown sacred tree. He did not smell an actual fragrance.

This verse is generally esteemed a masterpiece worthy of Bashō.

[65

花　　椿

落ざまに 水こぼしけり 花椿

芭　蕉

Hanatsubaki

Ochi-zama ni
Mizu koboshi-keri
Hanatsubaki

A Camellia Flower

Behold! a camellia flower
Spilt water when it fell.

Bashō

Imagine a camellia tree in full bloom. One of its blossoms dropped. The moment it dropped down, it spilt water. The water was yesterday's rain which had lodged in the blossom. A lovely verse portraying a refreshing incident on a fine morning after rain.

[66]

時　　鳥

はとゝぎす 消行く方や 島一つ

芭　蕉

Hototogisu

Hototogisu
Kieyuku kata ya
Shima hitotsu

The Cuckoo

Lo! there is an island
Where the cuckoo vanished from sight.

Bashō

This is a scene in the Inland Sea looked down upon from Mount Tekkai. A cuckoo, uttering its cry, has flown away. The startled poet follows the bird with his eye; and in the direction whither it has vanished he descries an island floating dimly like a dream—the Island of Awaji, which abounds in historic and poetic associations. This is an excellent realistic verse.

* * * * *

The hototogisu—
Fast vanishing from view,
Toward a solitary island.

Trans. by S. H. Wainright

[67]

芭　蕉

芭蕉植えて 先づにくむ荻の 二葉かな

芭　蕉

Bashō

Bashō uete
Mazu nikumu ogi no
Futaba kana

The Banana

I have planted a banana, and forthwith
Do hate young shoots of reed.

Bashō

It is a well known fact that in the garden of Bashō's hut in Fukagawa, Yedo, a banana was planted, whence the name of the hut, "Bashō-An," or "Banana Hermitage," and his pen name of "Bashō." When the poet planted the banana, he found some young shoots of reed growing in the garden. They were then small, but he was afraid they would grow large and thick and might torture his favourite plant. It is noteworthy that the strong words, "I hate," are very seldom employed in the verses of the large-hearted, mild-tempered poet.

[68]

大　井　川

五月雨の 雲吹きおとせ 大井川

芭　蕉

Ōi-Gawa

Samidare no
Kumo fuki-otose
Ōi-gawa

The Ōi River

Oh, mighty Ōi River,
Blow down those clouds of the May rains.

Bashō

On the way to his old home in Iga Province in May, 1694, Bashō was obliged to stay two or three days at the post-town of Shimada situated on the Ōi-gawa, famous for the swiftness of its current, the passage of which was then stopped by its high volume due to the May rains. Remember that in those days there were no iron bridges spanning such rapid rivers. The poet, impatiently waiting for the subsidence of the waters, addressed this verse to the mighty river flowing in torrents, requesting it to start a wind so as to blow away down the valley or river course the rain-fraught clouds which hung threateningly over it. Notice the interesting personification of the river and the powerful rhythm, fitting for the awful scene. A verse quite worthy of Bashō.

[**69**]

朝　　顔

朝顔や これもまた我 友ならず

芭　蕉

Asagao

Asagao ya
Kore mo mata waga
Tomo narazu

The Morning-Glory

Ah! the morning-glory!
'Tis not my friend, either.

Bashō

This verse, which is of a refreshingly simple and natural style, seems to suggest something profound, but it is impossible to make sure of the poet's meaning.

[70]

嵐雪におくる

さびしさを 問てくれぬか 桐一葉

芭　蕉

Ransetsu ni Okuru

Sabishisa wo
Tōte kurenuka
Kiri hitoha

To Ransetsu

Will you not call on me in my loneliness?
A paulownia leaf has fallen.

Bashō

"The fall of a paulownia leaf," in Japanese and Chinese literature, is a symbol of the dreariness and loneliness of autumn as well as the traditional saying, "The fall of a single leaf tells the arrival of autumn all over the world." Bashō means:—"A paulownia leaf has fallen in my garden, and lonesomeness overwhelms me. Will you please come and see me, my dear friend?"

I appreciate this verse which is a sincere outburst of his affectionate feelings toward his favourite pupil. It may here be parenthetically noted that Ransetsu and Kikaku were the poet's greatest favourites among his numerous pupils. On the one hand, it is true, Bashō was an ardent lover of nature and a so-called "nature poet"; but, on the other hand, he was a passionate lover of the human kind. He loved his pupils like his real children, which is the reason why he was regarded by them with a sort of filial piety.

[71]

柳 の 蝶

吹たびに 蝶の居直る 柳かな

芭 蕉

Yanagi no Chō

Fuku tabi ni
Chō no inaoru
Yanagi kana

A Butterfly on a Willow Tree

Lo! the butterfly shifts its seat
On the willow whenever the wind blows.

Bashō

A minute observation of a little, charming scene in sweet spring, and nothing else.

[72]

一笑を弔ふ

塚も動け 我泣聲は 秋の風

芭 蕉

Isshō wo Tomurō

Tsuka mo ugoke
Waga naku koe wa
Aki no kaze

On the Death of Isshō

Oh, grave-mound, move!
My wailing is the autumn wind.

Bashō

This verse is an elegy of Isshō, a poet of Kanazawa who, although not a personal pupil of Bashō, had a warm admiration for him and his poetry. He was comparatively young, but evinced a remarkable poetic talent. Therefore Bashō deeply lamented his premature death, and his feelings were powerfully excited. The result was this verse, which means:—"The autumn wind is my lamentation; therefore, grave-mound, move with it!" What a violent outburst of grief! Perhaps none but poets of Bashō's genius and sincerity can think of such impressive symbolism.

* * * * *

Shake! O tomb!
The sound of my wailing
Is the wind of autumn!

Trans. by Minoru Toyoda

[73]

鷗

水寒く 寝入かねたる かもめかな

芭　蕉

Kamome

Mizu samuku
Neiri kane taru
Kamome kana

The Sea Gull

The water is so cold,
The gull can hardly go to sleep.

Bashō

This verse was a greeting of thanks to a Buddhist priest named Genki (元起和尚) who had presented Bashō with a bottle of saké. It is a winter night and the water of the sea is so cold that a gull floating on it can hardly go to sleep. The implied meaning is that the poet himself can hardly go to sleep on account of the severe cold of night. Therefore he is very grateful to his kind friend. He will drink the saké and the resulting comfortable warmth will give him sweet sleep.

[74]

猿

初時雨 猿も小蓑を ほしげなり

芭　蕉

Saru

Hatsu-shigure
Saru mo ko-mino wo
Hoshige nari

The Monkey

The first drizzling shower is falling;
The monkey seems craving a small rain coat.
Bashō

This verse was so highly esteemed in Bashō's day that it was inserted at the beginning of an anthology and the anthology was entitled after it *Saru-Mino-Shū* or "The Monkey's Straw Rain Coat Collection." It was composed by Bashō in a mountain on the way to his old home of Ueno. *Shigure* is an intermittent drizzling rain in early winter. Well, the first drizzling shower was falling. Through the rain Bashō and his companion were trudging across a mountain. They caught sight of a monkey, soaked with the rain, sitting disconsolately on a branch or on a rock. They had on rain-outfit but the shivering animal had no protection and the compassionate poet thought it seemed to crave a small straw rain coat.

A sketch of a dreary mountain scene in rain.

[75]

鴨

海くれて 鴨の聲 ほのかにしろし

芭　蕉

Kamo

Umi kurete
Komo no koe
Honokani shiroshi

Wild Ducks

Night has fall'n on the sea.
Wild ducks' voices are faint and white.

Bashō

This excellent verse is believed to be a sketch of a scene in the sea of Owari. The curtain of darkling night had fallen on the sea, and the tops of white wavelets were faintly seen to rise and fall on the dim expanse. Through the darkness were audible the voices of wild ducks flying away out on the sea. The cacklings went farther and farther until they died away where white ripples were faintly visible. It is noteworthy that in this case Bashō thought it fitting to use the symbolic description " Wild ducks' voices are faint and white." Buson, the next greatest *haijin,* is also a symbolist in the following verse :—

Furu-ido ya
Kani tobu uwo no
Oto kurashi

'Tis an old well; dark is the sound
Of a fish leaping up at mosquitoes.

Bashō and Buson, in this respect, may be said to have forestalled modern symbolists. Some commentators aver that the rhythm of this verse, which consists of 5, 5, 7 syllables instead of the regular 5, 7, 5 is more appropriate for describing the lonely atmosphere of the cold dark sea of December; but unfortunately I cannot appreciate their reasoning. For my part, I prefer the smoother rhythm of the regular arrangement.

[**76**]

高 野 に て

父母の しきりに戀し 雉子の聲

芭 蕉

Kōya Nite

Chichi haha no
Shikirini koishi
Kiji no koe

On Kōya

Hearing a pheasant's cries,
How I longed for my dead parents!

Bashō

Kōya is a sacred mountain, the seat of a great Buddhist monastery, the head temple of the Shingon sect. On this sacred mountain a pheasant's cries broke the stillness on a sudden. As he listened to the shrill and plaintive cries, the poet was seized with lodgings for his dead parents. It is said that this pathetic verse was suggested by the famous sentence of a puppet play, *Yakeno no kigisu, yoru no tsuru, ko wo omowanu oya wa nashi*—"Whether be it a pheasant after a moorland fire or a crane at night, it all illustrates parental love for the young," and by Saint Gyōgi's poem:—

Horo horo to
Naku yamadori no
Koe kike ba
Chichi ka tozo omō
Haha ka tozo omō

Hearing a copper pheasant
Crying *horo horo,*
I fancy it to be
My father or mother.

[77]

月　と　雲

雲折々 人を休むる 月見かな

芭　蕉

Tsuki to Kumo

Kumo oriori
Hito wo yasumuru
Tsukimi kana

The Moon and Clouds

Clouds veil the moon now and again,
Giving rest to its beholders.

Bashō

A company of men are viewing the harvest moon. While they are absorbed in its contemplation, clouds veil the bright face of the moon now and then. During the interval they can give rest to their gazing eyes and enjoy a little chat. It is of course a great disappointment to have the harvest moon entirely shrouded in thick clouds; but to have it now and then veiled in a floating cloud is rather a joy to poets. Opinion is divided as to the merit of this verse. A commentator criticizes it adversely on the ground that it is unnatural in thought.

* * * * *

Oh! the moon-gazing, where some clouds
From time to time repose the eye!

Trans. by Basil Hall Chamberlain

Les nuages, de temps en temps,
Nous font reposer le cou,
Tandis que nous comtemplons la lune!

Traduit par Michel Revon

[78]

紅 の 花

行末は 誰が肌ふれん 紅の花

芭 蕉

Beni no Hana

Yukusue wa
Taga hada furen
Beni no hana

Rouge-Flowers

I wonder whose skin in future
Those rouge-flowers will touch!

Bashō

A dye-stuff made from the rouge-flower is often used for dyeing silk for women's underwear. At the sight of rouge-flowers the poet wonders what ladies' skin the silk dyed with a dye-stuff made from them will have the pleasure of touching in future.

This verse is not a good one but remarkable as the only suggestive ***haiku*** among Bashō's numerous verses.

[79]

訪 山 隱

橿の木の 花にかまはぬ すがたかな

芭 蕉

San-in wo Tou

Kashinoki no
Hana ni kamawanu
Sugata kana

When Visiting a Noble-Minded Recluse

The oak tree stands in majesty,
Regardless of the cherry-bloom!

Bashō

It is beyond doubt that the noble-minded recluse who lived secluded regardless of the vicissitudes of life, is likened to the hardy evergreen oak, which stands majestically as if it sets at naught the charming cherry-flowers, so highly esteemed but destined speedily to fade.

[80]

明 石 夜 泊

蛸壺や はかなき夢を 夏の月

芭 蕉

Akashi Yahaku

Tako-tsubo ya
Hakanaki yume wo
Natsu no tsuki

On Board a Ship off Akashi Bay

In its jar the octopus dreams
A brief dream 'neath the summer moon.

Bashō

At the bottom of the sea, bathed in the bright summer moon, there is an octopus-trap, consisting of a deep jar, in which the strange creature, quite innocent of its own danger, is perhaps dreaming a fleeting dream. The octopus is Bashō himself who, in spite of his fleeting life, was dreaming a sweet dream, quite snug in the ship. A beautiful rhythmical, rather humorous verse which suggests a melancholy view of life

* * * * *

Octopus pot, aye! and a brief dream
While the summer moon is shining.

Trans. by Basil Hall Chamberlain

[81]

二見の浦の畫を見て

うたがうな 潮の花も 浦の春

芭　蕉

Futami-no-Ura no E wo Mite

Utagōna
Ushio no hana mo
Ura no haru

On a Picture of Futami Bay

Doubt not! The bay, too, has its spring—
The flowerets of the rising tide.

Bashō

The waves breaking into beautiful white flower-like foam against the shore are among the charming spring sights of the bay. Never doubt it. Futami is a most picturesque place and few art motives are more popular than the *Myōto-Ishi,* or "Wife and Husband Rocks"—two rocks close to the shore. Notice that alliteration contributes to the melody of the verse:—*u*tagōna, *u*shio, *u*ra; *h*ana, *h*aru.

* * * * *

Do not doubt!
The flowers of the tide, too, are of
The Spring-time of the Bay.

Trans. by Minoru Toyoda

[82]

片野望翠亭にて

里ふりて 柿の木持たぬ 家もなし

芭 蕉

Katano Bōsui Tei Nite

Sato furite
Kakinoki motanu
Ie mo nashi

At Bōsui's House in Katano

The village is so old, there is
No house but has persimmon trees.

Bashō

The village where Bashō's pupil or friend, Bōsui, lived was a very old place, and therefore every house had some persimmon trees full of beautiful yellow or scarlet fruit. A purely objective sketch of a charming autumn scene in an old village, probably noted for persimmons.

[83]

さし竿書きたる扇に

鳥さしも 竿や捨てけむ 時鳥

芭　蕉

Sashizao Kakitaru Ōgi Ni

Torisashi mo
Sao ya suteken
Hototogisu

On a Fan Painted with a Bird-Catcher's Pole

A bird-catcher may have thrown away
His pole, hearing a cuckoo's sweet song.

Bashō

A bird-catcher, holding up his limed pole at a bird perched on a branch, may have thrown it away in bewildered ecstasy on hearing unexpectedly a cuckoo's sweet song.

[**84**]

日　光　山

あらたうと　青葉わかばの　日の光

芭　蕉

Nikkō-Zan

Ara tōto
Aoba wakaba no
Hi-no-hikari

On Mount Nikkō

How divine the sunbeams shining
On the young and green leaves!

Bashō

Mount Nikkō is noted for the mausoleums of the illustrious Shōgun Ieyasu and of his scarcely less famous grandson, Iemitsu, and a perfect assemblage of gorgeous shrines; for beautiful hills, cascades, immense forest trees, and particularly for the glorious tints of the autumn foliage and the young green foliage of early summer. In Bashō's day, when the Tokugawa Shōgun actually reigned, Mount Nikkō was a great centre of popular worship.

This verse was composed when Bashō worshipped at the Nikkō shrines. It was early summer and nothing seemed more divine to the pious poet than the sunbeams shining on the young green foliage of the whole mountain. This seemingly objective description implies the poet's reverence for the divine power. Doubtless "the divine sunbeams" refers to the name of Nikkō which signifies "Sunbeams." This verse cannot be called a masterpiece.

* * * * *

O, how august a spectacle meets my eye!
The sun upon fresh foliage far and nigh.

Trans. by Shigeru Nishimura

[85]

撫　子

酔うて寝む　撫子咲ける　石の上

芭　蕉

Nadeshiko

Yōte nen
Nadeshiko sakeru
Ishi no ue

The Pink

Oh! to drink deep and repose
On the stone over which the pinks bloom!

Bashō

The scene was probably the garden of Bashō's hut. Some pinks were blooming with profusion on a large stone. Fascinated by their beauty, the poet fancied humorously that he would like to get drunk with *saké* and take a sweet slumber on the stone. The poet's affinity with nature is noticeable.

[86]

案 山 子 の 袖

かりてねむ 案山子の袖や 夜半の霜

芭 蕉

Kagashi no Sode

Karite nen
Kagashi no sode ya
Yowa no shimo

The Sleeves of a Scarecrow

Would I might use the scarecrow's sleeves in sleep
As shelter from the midnight frost.

Bashō

A humorous, fanciful verse which requires no explanation.

[87]

奈 良 に て

菊の香や 奈良には古き 佛達

芭 蕉

Nara Nite

Kiku-no-ka ya
Nara niwa furuki
Hotoke tachi

At Nara

What fragrance of chrysanthemums at Nara!
How many ancient images of the Buddha!

Bashō

This verse was composed on the Chrysanthemum Festival day, September 9, 1694, when Bashō visited the ancient Imperial capital of Nara. There are in Nara numerous Buddhist temples with many wooden images of Buddha, of highly excellent workmanship, belonging to the Tempyō era. The poet visited one temple after another, and worshipped those ancient images with profound reverence. As he did so, a powerful fragrance of chrysanthemums floated through the air. Then he experienced an indescribable ecstasy, which spontaneously expressed itself in this beautiful verse.

[**88**]

園 女 亭 に て

しらぎくの 目に立てゝ見る 塵もなし

芭 蕉

Sono-Jo Tei Nite

Shiragiku no
Me ni tatete miru
Chiri mo nashi

At Madame Sono's Residence

Ah! on the white chrysanthemums,
Not even one speck to be seen!

Bashō

This beautiful verse was composed on September 26, 1694, when a poem party was held at the residence of Madame Sono, a pupil of Bashō, who lived at Ōsaka. It was ostensibly a eulogy on beautiful white chrysanthemus just in bloom in the garden, but the poet's purpose was to pay a tribute to the beauty and lofty character of his hostess.

[89]

時 鳥 の 聲

ほとゝぎす 聲横たふや 水の上

芭 蕉

Hototogisu no Koe

Hototogisu
Koe yokotō ya
Mizu no ue

The Cuckoo's Notes

Behold! the cuckoo's notes
Are trailing on the stream.

Bashō

The Japanese cuckoo is seldom visible and therefore its notes have been a frequent theme of poets from olden times. The present verse is an instance. It is a highly clever portrayal of a crying cuckoo flying across the water. The figurative phrase, " notes are trailing," is a vivid description of the bird's loud, shrill notes trailing like a shooting star across an expanse of water. " Behold ! " instead of " Hark ! " is used in accord with the above figure.

[**90**]

雲　雀

永き日を 囀り足らぬ 雲雀哉

芭　蕉

Hibari

Nagaki hi wo
Saezuri taranu
Hibari kana

The Skylark

The lark sings through the long spring day,
But never enough for its heart's content.

Bashō

The skylark sings untiringly through the long spring day, soaring through the hazy welkin, overlooking a picturesque field gay with green barley and golden rape-flowers. A verse worthy of an old hand. *Nagaki-hi,* or " the long day," in ***haiku*** means the long day of late spring, although, of course, the midsummer days are the longest of all.

*　*　*　*　*

Oh! skylark for whose carolling
The livelong day sufficeth not.

Trans. by Basil Hall Chamberlain

O tireless lark, the livelong day,
The longest summer day in all the year
Your song we never cease to hear.

Trans. by Curtis Hidden Page

Oh! l'alouette
Qui ne cesse de chanter
Toute la longue journée!

Traduit par Michel Revon

[91]

嵐 山 に て

花の山 二町登れば 大悲閣

芭 蕉

Arashiyama Nite

Hana no yama
Nichō noboreba
Daihi-Kaku

On Mount Arashi

Two *chō* up the hill of flowers,
Lo, the Daihi-Kaku Temple.

Bashō

A *chō* is about 120 metres. The hill of flowers means the hill covered with cherry-flowers. The Daihi-Kaku is a Buddhist temple dedicated to Kawannon, the Goddess of Mercy, who is reverentially addressed by Buddhists as *Daiji Daihi no Kwannon Sama* or "Oh! Goddess Kwannon of Great Mercy and Great Benevolence!" Hence the name of "The Daihi-Kaku" or "The Daihi Temple." This verse is a realistic description of Mount Arashi near Kyōto, celebrated for its cherry-flowers. At the foot of the hill (Arashi-yama is too low to be called a mountain) there is a stone monument inscribed with this verse. The verse means:—"When one has walked about two *chō* up the hill, contemplating the beautiful cherry-flowers, one finds an old temple dedicated to the Goddess of Mercy." At first sight the verse looks like a guide-post, but in reality it is an excellent *haiku* requiring a master's skill. *Hana-no-yama* or "the hill of flowers" is a beautiful phrase. The substitution of *Arashi-yama* for it would turn the verse into a prosaic indication of distance.

[92]

雪　見

いざ行かむ　雪見にころぶ　處まで

芭　蕉

Yukimi

Iza yukan
Yukimi ni korobu
Tokoro made

Snow-Viewing

Well, let's go snow-viewing,
Till we tumble over.

Bashō

Snow-viewing is a favourite pleasure with men of taste, particularly with poets.

This verse, be it rather a minor one, is interesting since it gives a peep into the frame of mind of the poet who devoted himself, soul and mind, to the contemplation of nature.

* * * * *

Maintenant, allons,
Jusqu'à l'endroit où
Nous tomberons, admirer la neige!

Traduit par Michel Revon

[93]

秋 深 し

秋深き 隣は何を する人ぞ

芭 蕉

Aki Fukashi

Aki fukaki
Tonari wa nani wo
Suru hito zo

Autumn is Advanced

The autumn is advanced.
What sort of people can my neighbours be?

Bashō

This verse was sent to a *haiku* party held at the residence of an Ōsaka pupil, which Bashō was unable to attend, lying in bed with a serious illness to which he succumbed a fortnight later. *Fukaki* is spelt *fukashi* in most books but the former spelling is right. The bedridden poet muses:—The autumn is advanced and a dreary and lonesome atmosphere reigns. But the neighbours' house is particularly quiet. It is silent as the grave. What can they be? How do they spend this dreary autumn?

Some commentators consider this verse a mystic, profound piece revealing the depths of the poet's soul.

[**94**]

茶 摘 と 時 鳥

木がくれて 茶摘も聞くや ほとゝぎす

芭 蕉

Chatsumi to Hototogisu

Kogakurete
Chatsumi mo kiku ya
Hototogisu

Tea-Pickers and a Cuckoo

It may be that, hidden in the shade of the trees,
Tea-pickers too are listening to the cuckoo.

Bashō

This was probably composed at Uji situated at an easy distance from Kyōto, noted for the production of excellent tea. Imagine Bashō walking leisurely through some tea plantations one fine day of early summer. Unexpectedly, overhead, a cuckoo cried on the wing. He listened with delighted surprise, and fancied that even the people picking tea might be listening to the bird, hiding themselves in the shade of the trees.

[95]

示二門人一

子に飽と 申す人には 花もなし

芭蕉

Monjin ni Shimesu

Ko ni aku to
Mōsu hito niwa
Hana mo nashi

Shown to a Pupil

There are no cherry-flowers for those men
Who say that they are tired of their children.

Bashō

It is probable that this verse was shown to a pupil who complained "Bringing up my children gives me much trouble and anxiety. They are quite a nuisance to me!" Bashō's precept means, "A man who is tired of his children cannot find any joy in the sight of charming cherry-flowers. Why, a child is a flower, so to speak." On the one hand, this verse was a precept; on the other, it suggested the poet's attitude toward his pupils at large, who were in a sense his children. He was not tired at all of teaching them; nay, he found in their instruction just the same joy that he found in cherry-flowers.

[96]

棉　　畠

名月{の/や} 花かと 見えて棉畠

芭　蕉

Wata-Batake

Meigetsu {*no* / *ya*}
Hana ka to miete
Wata-batake

A Cotton Field

What looked like flowers in the bright moonlight
Is nothing but a cotton field.

Bashō

In the bright moonlight the white, fibrous substance clothing the seeds of the cotton plants glistens beautifully like a mass of white cherry-flowers. What an enchanting sight! This simple realistic verse is rather remarkable for the poetical rendering of a prosaic theme.

*　*　*　*　*

Au brillant clair de lune
Ce qui semblait être des fleurs,
C'est un champ de cotonniers.

Traduit par Michel Revon

[97]

草庵にて

花の雲　鐘は上野か　淺草か

芭蕉

Sōan Nite

Hana no kumo
Kane wa Ueno ka
Asakusa ka

At My Hut

A cloud of flowers! An evening bell booms.
At Ueno or at Asakusa?

Bashō

One of Bashō's most famous verses, and quite a masterpiece. The theme is a distant view of the cherry-blossoms on both banks of the Sumida River, seen from the poet's hut situated about a mile below. Remember that in Bashō's day in that neighbourhood there were very few houses obstructing the view.

It is a rather warm spring afternoon. Mukōjima, Ueno and Asakusa are wrapt in clouds of cherry-blossoms veiled in a thin haze. The poet, casting his gaze out of the window, is spellbound by the sight. At that moment the boom of a great evening bell resounds through the flowers and the haze. He wonders whether the bell is that of the Kwan-eiji Temple at Ueno or that of the Sen-sōji Temple at Asakusa—both famous Buddhist temples.

* * * * *

A cloud of flowers!
Is the bell Ueno
Or Asakusa?

Trans. by W. G. Aston

A cloud of blossoms
Far and near;
Then sweet and clear,
What bell is that
That charms my ear?
    Ueno?
        Asakusa?

Trans. by Clara A. Walsh

Par les nuages de fleurs,
La cloche; est-ce celle d'Ouéno,
Ou celle d'Açakouça?

Traduit par Michel Revon

[98]

草 庵 の 月 見

名月や 池をめぐりて 夜もすがら

芭 蕉

Sōan no Tsukimi

Meigetsu ya
    Ike wo megurite
        Yomosugara

Moon-Viewing at My Hut

Oh, glorious moon! I strolled
Around the pond all night long.

Bashō

"This verse looks commonplace but is by no means commonplace;" says Rohan, an authority on poetry, "its meaning needs no explanation."

The poem reveals Bashō's absorption in nature.

[99]

行 く 春

行く春に　和歌の浦にて　追付たり

芭　蕉

Yuku Haru

Yuku haru ni
Waka-no-ura nite
Oitsuki tari

Departing Spring

I have caught up departing Spring
Here at the Bay of Waka-no-ura.

Bashō

The last days of Spring are called *Yuku haru* or "departing Spring." Waka-no-ura Bay, in the province of Kii, is noted for beautiful views, a mild temperature and literary associations. "Poets have sung the beauty of this spot ever since Japan has had a literature." Bashō had met Spring on Mount Yoshino and Mount Kōya before he came to Waka-no-ura; but on those places he had been depressed by too melancholy thoughts to enjoy it. Here at Waka-no-ura, to his delighted surprise, he found Spring still lingering with her flowers, verdure, sweet birds and soft, fragrant breezes; and furthermore the picturesque scenery welcomed him smilingly. Now for the first time he experienced the joy of the season and felt as if he had overtaken the departing Spring of which he had been in pursuit. Unquestionably, a beautiful verse.

[100]

檜　笠

芳野にて　櫻見せうぞ　檜笠

芭　蕉

Hinoki-Gasa

Yoshino nite
Sakura mishōzo
Hinoki-gasa

The *Hinoki-Gasa*

My dear hat, I will let you see
The cherry-bloom at Yoshino.

Bashō

A *hinoki-gasa* is a large basket-work hat made of small thin pieces of *hinoki* (Japanese cypress) wood. This kind of hat was worn generally by Buddhist ascetics in olden days.

In March, 1688, Bashō, accompanied by his favourite pupil Tokoku, visited Mount Yoshino celebrated for its cherry-blossoms and its historic associations. Just previous to the trip, on the tiptoe of delightful expectancy, the poet burst into verse and penned the above on the inside of his *hinoki*-hat. Tokoku also wrote the following verse on the inside of his hat.

芳野にて 我も見せうぞ 檜笠

Yoshino nite
Ware mo mishōzo
Hinoki-gasa

My hat, I too will let you see
The cherry-bloom at Yoshino.

[**101**]

小 さ き 蚊

わが宿は 蚊のちいさきを 馳走かな

芭　蕉

Chiisaki Ka

Waga yado wa
Ka no chiisaki wo
Chisō kana

Small Mosquitoes

In my cottage the mosquitoes are small;
That is all the good cheer I can offer.

Bashō

This rather humorous verse was shown to a pupil of Bashō named Aki-no-Bō, a Buddhist priest of Kanazawa, when the latter called at his temporary residence "Genjū-An" near Lake Biwa. Bashō means:—"My dear friend, you are welcome at my cottage. I'm sorry I can offer you no dainties, but the mosquitoes here are small and don't bite much. That is the only good cheer I can offer you."

This verse is interesting as it well represents the poet's simple life.

[102]

多田の社にて實盛がかぶとを見て

むざんやな 甲の下の きりぎりす

芭　蕉

Tada-no-Yashiro nite Sanemori ga Kabuto wo Mite

Muzan yana
Kabuto no shita no
Kirigirisu

On Sanemori's Helmet which I Saw at the Tada Shrine

Alas! beneath the helmet
A grasshopper is chirruping.

Bashō

The Chinese character for "helmet" is 冑 or 兜 not 甲 which even Bashō misused. Saitō Sanemori was a famous warrior of the Taira family, who fell fighting bravely in a battle fought against the Minamoto family. The veteran soldier, over seventy years old, tradition says, dyed his hair before he went to the battle. Among the treasures of the Tada Shrine at the town of Komatsu, in Kaga Province, there is an old beautiful helmet which is said to have been worn by Sanemori at his last battle.

During his journey through the northwestern provinces, Bashō visited the Tada Shrine and, seeing the helmet in question, burst into the above pathetic verse which is, needless to say, a dirge on the old warrior's tragic fate. It seems likely that the grasshopper was chirruping close to the shrine, but Bashō says "under the helmet" for poetic effect.

* * * * *

Alas, the ancient warrior's tragic fate!
Under his helmet chirps a cricket late.

Trans. by Shigeru Nishimura

[103]

富士の風

富士の風や　扇にのせて　江戸土産

芭　蕉

Fuji no Kaza

Fuji no kaze ya
Ōgi ni nosete
Yedo miyage

The Wind of Mount Fuji

**Would that I could put Mt. Fuji's wind on my fan,
And take it back to Yedo as a souvenir-gift.**

Bashō

A humorous panegyric of the refreshing wind blowing down the peerless mountain.

[104]

蟬 の 聲

閑さや 岩にしみいる 蟬の聲

芭 蕉

Semi no Koe

Shizukasa ya
Iwa ni shimi-iru
Semi no koe

Cicadas' Voices

**What stillness! The cicadas' voices
Penetrate the rocks.**

Bashō

This verse was inspired when Bashō visited the Ryūshakuji Temple, situated near the city of Yamagata. The temple is a beautiful building, among ancient pines and oaks, on a pile of numerous mossy, gigantic rocks. It appears that the poet visited the place near sunset. How quiet the temple and its neighbourhood were! The cicadas cried *jii-jii* in a rather low, monotonous tone. Their voices sounded as if they penetrated and pervaded the rocks. Strange to say, two or three cicadas' comparatively low voices heard in a quiet spot sometimes give an impression of stillness. The figurative language "penetrated the rocks" is precisely right and worthy of a wonderful genius.

This is quite a masterpiece and one of Bashō's best known *haiku.*

* * * * *

How silent!
The cicadas' shrill
Sinks into the rocks.

Trans. by Minoru Toyoda

The utter silence—
And sinking straight into the rocks,
A cicada's shrill.

Trans. by Glenn Shaw

[105]

雲雀と雉子

雲雀鳴く 中の柏子や 雉子の聲

芭 蕉

Hibari to Kiji

Hibari naku
Nakano hyōshi ya
Kiji no koe

The Skylark and the Pheasant

While merrily the skylarks sing,
Pheasants' cries mark time, now and then.

Bashō

The skylarks are constantly singing sweetly, while now and then the shrill cries of pheasants are heard. The pheasants' cries sound as if they mark time with the sweet songs of the skylarks.

A clever description of an ethereal music.

[106]

畫　讃

白露を　こぼさぬ萩の　うねりかな

芭　蕉

Gwasan

Shira-tsuyu wo
Kobosanu hagi no
Uneri kana

On a Picture

The lespedeza flowers sway and sway,
But not enough to shake down their white dews.

Bashō

The *hagi* or lespedeza is an autumn herb with graceful pliant stems and little lovely flowers, either red or white.

A beautiful verse quite worthy of the graceful flower.

* * * * *

Ah! the waving lespedeza,
Which spills not a drop
Of the clear dew!

Trans. by W. G. Aston

[107]

年 く れ ぬ

年くれぬ 笠著て草鞋 はきながら

芭　蕉

Toshi Kurenu

Toshi kurenu
Kasa kite waraji
Hakinagara

The Year Has Drawn to a Close

Ah! the year has come to an end while still
I am wearing my hat and straw sandals.

Bashō

A verse which symbolizes Bashō's life and usual frame of mind. It is in itself a picture of the itinerant poet who, in hat and sandals, bids farewell to one year and hails another.

[108]

所　　思

此の道や 行く人なしに 秋のくれ

芭　蕉

Shoshi

Kono michi ya
Yuku hito nashi ni
Aki no kure

My Thoughts

None goes along this way but I,
This autumn eve.

Bashō

This was composed in September, 1694, Bashō's last year, at a tea house in the suburbs of Ōsaka. It was an autumn evening. In front of the tea house in question there lay a long highway, as far as eye could reach. Along it not a soul was to be seen, except the poet himself. What a lonesome evening!

Such is the surface meaning, but the implied meaning is generally conjectured to be as follows:—The *haikai* world at large was dreary and lonesome like an autumn evening. The poet was afraid none of his pupils would be able to follow in his wake on the path of poetry.

[109]

故主蟬吟公の庭前にて

さまざまの 事おもひ出す 櫻かな

芭　蕉

Koshu Sengin-Kō no Teizen Nite

Samazama no
Koto omoi-dasu
Sakura kana

At the Garden of my Departed Master, Lord Sengin

Ah! the cherry-blossoms
Have brought many memories back.

Bashō

During his stay at his old home in December, 1687, Bashō was invited by his dead Lord Sengin's son to a cherry-viewing party. At sight of the cherry-blossoms in the garden of his lord who had died twenty years before, the poet's heart was full of profound emotion. The result was the above verse.

[110]

唇 寒 し (座右の銘。人の短をいふ事なかれ。己が長を說くこと勿れ。)

物言へば 唇寒し 秋の風

芭 蕉

Kuchibiru Samushi

(***Zayū no Mei. Hito no tan wo yū koto nakare. Onore ga chō wo toku koto nakare.***)

Mono-ieba
Kuchibiru samushi
Aki no kaze

My Lips Feel Cold

(My motto :—Never speak of another man's faults or of your own virtues.)

When I speak, my lips feel cold,
The autumn wind blowing.

Bashō

A didactic verse which means :—"Keep silence, otherwise evil will overtake you." This verse is so popularly known that when a man regrets having spoken he often quotes it.

It is almost a proverb among educated people.

[111]

門弟猿雖に與ふ

もろもろの 心柳に まかすべし

芭　蕉

Montei Ensui ni Atō

Moromoro no
Kokoro yanagi ni
Makasu beshi

Given to My Pupil Ensui

Yield to the willow
All passions, all desires of your heart.

Bashō

Let not your mind be burdened with passions, evil thoughts and undue ambitions, but endeavour always to keep it calm and serene, just as the pliable willow does not resist the wind but keeps itself safe and peaceful. "Yield to the willow" is an ingenious figure of speech.

[112]

光　　堂

五月雨の 降り殘してや 光堂

芭　蕉

Hikari-Dō

Samidare no
Furi nokoshite-ya
Hikari-dō

The "Shining Hall"

It seems the heavy rains of May
Have left the "Shining Hall" untouched.
Bashō

The *Hikari-dō* or "Shining Hall," whose proper name is the *Konjiki-dō* or "Golden Hall," belongs to the Chūsonji, a famous Buddhist temple at Hiraizumi, in the province of Rikuchū, built by the Fujiwaras, a powerful warrior family who ruled the northeastern provinces in the twelfth century. The "Shining Hall" is dedicated to the three deities, Amida, Kwannon and Seishi, and contains the coffins of three Fujiwara generals. Its columns are inlaid with rich jewels and its interior is entirely gilt, so that it shines with dazzling brilliance. Hence its popular name of the "Shining Hall." In the early summer of 1689 Bashō visited the ruins of the Fujiwaras' castle and the Chūsonji Temple at Hiraizumi. Struck with the beauty and brilliancy of the "Shining Hall," he burst into the above verse which means:—"Even the heavy rains of May during several centuries seem to have failed to drench and injure the hall, so that it still continues to shine as brilliantly as ever."

[113]

雨 の 富 士

霧時雨 富士を見ぬ日ぞ おもしろき

芭　蕉

Ame no Fuji

Kiri-shigure
Fuji wo minu hi zo
Omoshiroki

Mount Fuji in Rain

A day when Fuji is unseen,
Veiled in a misty winter shower —
That day, too, is a joy.

Bashō

This was inspired when Bashō was crossing the Hakone hills on a winter day. The peerless mountain which he had expected to see was unfortunately veiled in a misty shower; but instead of being disappointed, the nature poet rather enjoyed the sight without Fuji. None but a poet of Bashō's temperament can have such feelings.

[**114**]

蟬　の　殼

聲に皆　鳴しまうてや　蟬の殼

芭　蕉

Semi no Kara

Koe ni mina
Naki shimōte-ya
Semi no kara

The Shell of a Cicada

Its body consumed, haply by crying,
There remains only the cicada's shell.

Bashō

A fanciful idea. The verse is not of high value.

* * * * *

The voice having been all consumed by crying, there remains only the shell of the *semi*.

Trans. by Lafcadio Hearn

[115]

明 照 寺 の 庭

百年の 氣色を庭の 落葉かな

芭 蕉

Myōshō-Ji no Niwa

Hyakunen no
Keshiki wo niwa no
Ochiba kana

The Garden of the Myōshōji Temple

The garden has a century-old air;
And lo! 'tis strewn with fallen leaves.

Bashō

When Bashō called on his pupil, Abbot Riyū, at his temple, the Myōshōji, in the vicinty of Hikone in the province of Ōmi, the temple was a century old since it had been removed there from its former site.

The temple being already a hundred years old, its garden is perfect, with mossy rocks and stately trees. Moreover, fallen leaves strewn over the garden add to its old world air.

* * * * *

A hundred years and more,
Each year has cast its withered leaves
My little garden o'er.

Trans. by William N. Porter

[116]

雪 丸 げ

君火をたけ よき物見せん 雪丸げ

芭 蕉

Yuki-Maroge

Kimi hi wo take
Yoki mono misen
Yuki-maroge

A Ball of Snow

Friend, make a fire. I'll let you see
Something lovely—a ball of snow.

Bashō

This verse was addressed to Sora, a faithful pupil and friend of Bashō, who lived in the immediate neighbourhood of his hut in Fukagawa. Sora called morning and evening to assist him in domestic work. One snowy evening he called as usual. The poet, who, like a little boy, had been playing with the snow in his garden, was much delighted. "So glad to see you, Sora!" said he playfully, "Would you make a fire and prepare tea? I have something nice to show you. What do you guess it is? Why, it is a beautiful big ball of snow." Probably such a remark was turned into the above humorous verse, which, though it is a trifling piece, is interesting as a spontaneous manifestation of the innocent poet's affectionate feelings toward his pupil.

[117]

旅 に 病 で

旅に病で 夢は枯野を かけめぐる

芭　蕉

Tabi ni Yande

Tabi ni yande
Yume wa kareno wo
Kake meguru

Taken Ill While Travelling

(A) **I'm taken ill while travelling;**
And my dreams roam o'er withered moors.

(B) **Taken ill on my travels,**
My dreams roam over withered moors.

Bashō

I have spent almost all my life in travelling. Now I am taken ill on my journey, but my dreams, carrying my soul on them, travel freely like birds. Every spot they convey me to is a desolate, withered moor. I am truding over withered moors in my travelling attire. Now I find myself on a moor of Owari Province, then on a moor of Mino Province.

This verse spontaneously reveals Bashō's habitual mood as an itinerant poet, who was quite content with his wandering life, thoroughly absorbed in the contemplation of nature, and heartily enjoyed a life of loneliness and refinement. It is a beautiful poem with a powerful rhythm and a bold figure of speech. I highly appreciate the personification of "dreams." "My dreams roam......," not "I roam in dreams," is a supreme expression.

* * * * *

Ta'en ill while journeying, I dreamt
I wandered o'er a withered moor.

Trans. by Basil Hall Chamberlain

At midway of my journey fallen ill,
To-night I fare again,
In dream, across a desert plain.

Trans. by Curtis Hidden Page

Lying ill on journey,
Ah, my dreams
Run about the ruin of fields.

Trans. by Yone Noguchi

Nearing my journey's end,
In dreams I trudge the wild waste moor,
And seek a kindly friend.

Trans. by William N. Porter

On a journey ta'en ill—
My dream a dried-up plain,
Through which I wander.

Trans. by Glenn Shaw

Tombé malade en voyage,
En rêve, sur une plaine déserte
Je me promène!

Traduit par Michel Revon

[118]

近 江 八 景

七景は 霧に隠れて 三井の鐘

芭 蕉 (?)

Ōmi Hakkei

Shichikei wa
Kiri ni kakurete
Mii no kane

The Eight Views of Ōmi

The seven views deep hidden in the mist
The evening bell of the Mii Temple booms.

Bashō (?)

Lake Biwa in Ōmi Province, the largest lake in Japan, is noted for the s
called *Ōmi Hakkei* or the "Eight Views of Ōmi," which are the Autumn Mo

seen from Ishiyama (石山秋月), the Evening Snow on Hirayama (比良暮雪), the Blaze of Evening at Seta (瀬田夕照), the Evening Bell of Miidera (三井晩鐘), the Boats Sailing Back from Yabashi (矢橋歸帆), a Bright Sky with a Breeze at Awazu (粟津晴嵐), the Rain by Night at Karasaki (唐崎夜雨) and the Wild Geese Alighting at Katata (堅田落雁).

A man of Ōmi Province, tradition says, once asked Bashō to write a *haiku* dealing with the "Eight Views of Ōmi." It was perhaps the hardest task that has ever embarrassed any poet; why, even mentioning the names of the "Eight Views" would require at least sixty syllables! After a few moments' reflection, the resourceful poet composed the above verse, which astonished the Ōmi man.

* * * * *

O Temple Bell of Mii!
Thy soothing sound
Now hides behind the haze
Those seven lovely views.

Trans. by Gonnosuke Komai

西　鶴 (姓—井原)
元祿六年歿　享年五十二
Saikaku (surname, Ibara)
A novelist and a poet; Sō-in's pupil in *haikai* (1641–1693)

[**119**]

更　　衣

長持に　春ぞくれ行く　更衣

西　鶴

Koromo-gae

Nagamochi ni
Haru zo kure-yuku
Koromo-gae

The Change of Garments

At the change of garments,
Spring disappears into the chest.

Saikaku

In most books *Haru zo kure-yuku* is misspelt *Haru kakure-yuku.*

In Old Japan on the first of April of the lunar calendar (the present May), spring suits were changed for summer suits and the heavier clothes were stowed away in long chests. This custom was called *koromo-gae* or "the change of garments."

When spring garments were changed for summer ones, the merry, beautiful spring came to a close and the hot summer set in; in other words, "Spring disappeared into the long chest"—a witty, humorous conceit, typical of Saikaku, who was a greater novelist than *haijin.*

* * * * *

A change of garments, and the spring
Goes into hiding in the chest.

Trans. by Basil Hall Chamberlain

[120]

けふの月

鯛は花は 見ぬ里もあり けふの月

西鶴

Kyō no Tsuki

Tai wa hana wa
Minu sato mo ari
Kyō no tsuki

To-night's Moon

Some villages have no sea-breams, no flowers;
But to-night's moon is seen in all villages.

Saikaku

There may be some villages which cannot taste the sea-bream, the nicest of fish, or cannot enjoy the sight of cherry-blossoms, the most beautiful of flowers; but the charming blessing of the harvest moon is enjoyed impartially by all the villages throughout Japan.

[121]

辞世

浮世の月 見過しにけり 末二年

西鶴

Jisei

Ukiyo no tsuki
Misugoshi ni keri
Sue ninen

The Death Verse

I have enjoyed the harvest moon
Two extra years in fleeting life.

Saikaku

In Japan a man's allotted life is counted as fifty years. Therefore Saikaku, who lived to the age of fifty-two, considered his last two years to be extra ones.

A *jisei* (辭世) or " death verse " was written on the death-bed by a person of literary taste: a custom of Old Japan.

素　堂 (姓一山口)
享保元年歿　享年七十五
Sodō (surname, Yamaguchi)
A native of Kai Province; lived in Yedo; Kigin's pupil (1641–1716)

[122]

春

宿の春 何もなきこそ 何もあれ

素　堂

Haru

Yado no haru
Nani mo naki koso
Nani mo are

Spring

In my hut, this New Year time, there's nothing,
Which means that in it there is everything.

Sodō

The New Year has called at my hut. But in it there is nothing appropriate to the season. Ah! I am wrong. That there is nothing is after all the same as that there is everything, and therefore I can feel the joy of Spring all the same.

The paradox means that a man's happiness does not depend so much on outward circumstances as on his attitude toward them. This verse well mirrors the sentiments of a poet who is indifferent to worldly pleasures.

[**123**]

燒　石

夕立に 燒石涼し 淺間山

素　堂

Yakeishi

Yūdachi ni
Yakeishi suzushi
Asama-yama

Lava

A summer shower having passed,
How cool the lava on Mount Asama!

Sodō

Asama-yama (8,280 ft.) near Karuizawa in Shinano Province is the largest active volcano in Japan.

The volcano loomed terrible with its column of smoke, its colourless grasses and ugly lava burning hot to the touch in the summer sun. Suddenly came a heavy shower and soon passed over. Then, what a change! The drenched lava was cool and refreshing and the mountain looked smiling. A delightful verse.

[**124**]

我　影

我をつれて　我かげ歸る　月見かな

素　堂

Waga Kage

Ware wo tsurete
Waga kage kaeru
Tsukimi kana

My Shadow

What a bright harvest moon!
My shadow walks home with me.

Sodō

The poet is walking home in the bright beams of the harvest moon. His shadow is cast on the ground in front of him. In other words, his shadow is walking home accompanied by him. An exquisite night scene!

[125]

胡蘿蔔(にんじん)の花

たれか見ん　櫻の頃の　野人蔘

素　堂

Ninjin no Hana

Tare ka min
Sakura no koro no
Noninjin

The Wild Carrot Flowers

Who cares to look at the wild carrot flowers
When the cherry-blossoms are in their glory?

Sodō

[126]

西　瓜

西瓜ひとり　野分を知らぬ　あしたかな

素　堂

Suika

Suikwa hitori
Nowaki wo shiranu
Ashita kana

The Water-Melon

The water-melons alone sit serene,
Quite unaware of last night's storm.

Sodō

Ashita as a poetic expression means "morning," while it means "to-morrow" as a colloquial word.

Last night there was a tempest working devastation all round. But this morning the water-melons alone are sitting calm and uninjured, as if they knew not of the storm.

來　山 (姓一小西)
享保元年歿　享年六十三
Raizan (surname, Konishi)
An Ōsaka man and Sō-in's pupil (1653–1716)

[**127**]

大阪も大阪まん中に住んで
お奉行の 名さへ覺えず 年暮れぬ

來　山

Ōsaka mo Ōsaka Mannaka ni Sunde

O-Bugyō no
Na sae oboezu
Toshi kure nu

Even Living in the Very Heart of Ōsaka

The year had gone before I learned the name
Of His Excellency the Governor.

Raizan

The *Bugyō* of Ōsaka was its Mayor, invested with executive and judicial ›wers.

The poet was so much absorbed in a life of solitary culture that he did not arn even the name of the chief magistrate of Ōsaka, although he lived in its ›ry heart.

[128]

白　　魚

白魚や さながら動く 水の{魂/色}

來　山

Shira-uwo

Shira-uwo ya
Sanagara ugoku
Mizu no {tama/iro}

The Whitebait

The whitebait looks as if
The {soul / colour} of the water moves.

Raizan

Of the two readings of the last line, *tama* (魂) or "soul" is superior to *iro* (色) or "colour."

The *shira-uwo,* a kind of whitebait, is a lovely, transparent, small fish valued as food. This verse is quite a masterpiece.

[129]

愛兒を失ひて

春の夢 氣の違はぬが 恨めしい

來 山

Aiji wo Ushinaite

Haru no yume
Ki no chigawanu ga
Urameshii

On the Death of a Beloved Child

Life is fleeting as a spring dream.
What a pity I haven't gone mad!

Raizan

Alas! my son is dead. How short and sweet his life was! It was as brief as a spring night' dream. If I had gone mad, I should not be conscious of this sorrow.

Remember that in Japanese literature fleeting life is often likened to a spring night's dream. Here it is especially appropriate.

[130]

櫻 さ く

花さいて 死とむないが 病哉

來 山

Sakura Saku

Hana saite
Shini tomu nai ga
Yamai kana

Cherry-Blossoms Come Out

The cherry-blossoms coming out,
I hate to die; but ah! I'm ill.

Raizan

The poet had been seriously ill and was quite prepared for death; but on the appearance of cherry-blossoms, ardent longings for Nature seized his mind and he hated to die.

言　水（姓—池西）
享保七年歿　享年七十三
Gonsui (surname, Ikenishi)
A native of Nara; Shigeyori's pupil (1649–1722)

[**131**]

木　　枯

木枯の　果はありけり　海の音

言　水

Kogarashi

Kogarashi no
Hate wa ari keri
Umi no oto

The Bleak Wind

The raging bleak wind died away,
Till it remained as the sound of the sea.

Gonsui

It was in early winter. All day long a bleak wind raged, as if it would blow for ever. In the evening a sound of sea waves began to be heard. The wind had abated. The roar of the sea grew louder by degrees until the sound of the wind was entirely swallowed in the sound of the sea. The wind had died away.

This verse was so popular in the poet's day that he acquired the nickname of "Kogarashi no Gonsui," or "Gonsui of the Bleak Wind."

[132]

風　鈴

吹かぬ日の　風鈴は蜂の　やどりかな

言　水

Fukanu hi no
Fūrin wa hachi no
Yadori kana

A Wind-Bell

A wind-bell on a windless day
Is just a shelter for the bees.

Gonsui

A *fūrin* (風鈴) or "wind-bell" is a tiny bell about an inch in height, whose office it is to produce a delightfully cool wind by the action of its tongue, swayed by a long strip of artistic stiff paper often inscribed with a verse, which flutters gently in the wind. Such bells are often hung on the eaves in summer by people of refined taste.

The wind-bell which does not ring on a windless day gives a shelter for bees.

[133]

嵯　峨　に　て

淺ましや　蟲なく中に　尼一人

來　山

Saga Nite

Asamashi ya
Mushi naku naka ni
Ama hitori

At Saga

How melancholy! A nun stands alone,
Amid the insects sadly chirruping.

Raizan

The village of Saga near Kyōto is noted for its many Buddhist temples and convents.

What a pathetic picture! a nun walking alone in an autumn field, where insects are chirruping sadly.

鬼　貫（姓—上島）
元文三年歿　享年七十八
Onitsura (surname, Kamijima)
A native of Itami; Sō-in's pupil
(1660–1738)

[**134**]

園　城　寺

花散つて　又しづかなり　園城寺

鬼　貫

Onjō-Ji

Hana chitte
Mata shizuka nari
Onjō-ji

The Onjōji Temple

The cherry-flowers having gone,
Onjōji Temple is quiet again.

Onitsura

In the cherry-blossom season, the temple was crowded with flower-viewers and worshippers. On the disappearance of the flowers, the temple was restored to its former atmosphere of quietude and holiness.

The Onjōji Temple, near Lake Biwa, is the same as the Miidera Temple mentioned above. The "Miidera Temple" is its popular name.

[135]

名月と亡児

此秋は 膝に子の無き 月見かな

鬼貫

Meigetsu to Bōji

Kono aki wa
Hiza ni ko no naki
Tsukimi kana

The Harvest Moon and a Dead Child

Alas! I view this autumn's moon
Without my baby on my lap.

Onitsura

[136]

花　　見

骸骨の　上を装ふて　花見かな

鬼　貫

Hanami

Gaikotsu no
Ue wo yosōte
Hanami kana

Flower-Viewing

The people view the cherry-bloom,
Their skeletons wrapt in rich silks.

Onitsura

In the cherry-blossom season all people, high and low, young and old, rich and poor, go flower-viewing, dressed in their finest clothes. Under the flowers some of them dance and others drink and sing. Each and all give themselves up to merriment. But alas! under their fineries are to be found their ghastly skeletons. To-day's joy will turn to-morrow's sorrow. Death comes to all. Life is an empty dream.

This verse, although very famous, seems to be of little value.

*   *   *   *   *

Oh! flower-gazers, who have decked
The surface of their skeletons!

Trans. by Basil Hall Chamberlain

De leurs squelettes
Le dessus ayant couvert,
Contemplation des fleurs!

Traduit par Michel Revon

[137]

更　衣

戀のない 身にも嬉しや 更衣

鬼　貫

Koromo-gae

Koi no nai
Mi nimo ureshi ya
Koromo-gae

The Change of Garments

Even I who have no sweetheart
Rejoice at the change of garments.

Onitsura

[138]

鶯

鶯や 音を入れてただ 青い鳥

鬼 貫

Uguisu

Uguisu ya
Ne wo irete tada
Aoi tori

The Nightingale

The nightingale, ceasing to sing,
Is nothing, alas, but a green bird.

Onitsura

The *uguisu* or Japanese nightingale is the sweetest of Japanese songsters, but it is not particularly beautiful to look at. It sings sweetly in February and March; and although it sometimes twitters in summer and even in winter, its notes are not then sweet. Therefore the nightingale is generally said to cease to sing in early summer.

[139]

行 水

行水の 捨てどころなき 蟲の聲

鬼 貫

Gyōzui

Gyōzui no
Sute dokoro naki
Mushi no koe

Bath Water

Nowhere can I throw away the bath water,
Insects singing sweetly all around.

Onitsura

In most books *naki* is misspelt *nashi.*

In the evening during the hottest time of summer, common people, particularly country people, often take a hot bath in small tubs in the open air. *Gyōzui* means this custom and the bath water too.

When summer is advanced and autumn draws near, insects are heard to chirrup sweetly in gardens and fields.

One evening the poet had taken his open air bath and was about to throw away the water. But insects were singing sweetly all round in the grasses and under the trees, so he was puzzled where to throw the water away, lest he might hurt the charming singers.

A beautiful verse, perhaps the best of Onitsura's *haiku.*

[140]

冬 と 夏

冬はまた 夏がましじやと {言はれけり / いひにけり}

鬼 貫

Fuyu to Natsu

Fuyu wa mata
Natsu ga mashi ja to
{Iware keri
{Ii ni keri

Winter and Summer

In winter men say,
Summer is better.

Onitsura

Iware keri and *iini keri* mean the same thing.
A didactic verse of little value.

* * * * *

While it's summer people say
Winter is the better season.
Such is human reason!

Trans. by Curtis Hidden Page

And in the summer, folks opined
That winter was to be preferred.

Trans. by Basil Hall Chamberlain

The last line of Page's translation is quite superfluous. This translation, minus the last line, is excellent, though the seasons' names are transposed.

L'été, de nouveau :
" L'hiver est préférable,"
Disait-on.

Traduit par Michel Revon

[141]

け ふ の 月

筆とらぬ 人もあらうか けふの月

鬼 貫

Kyō no Tsuki

Fude toranu
Hito mo arōka
Kyō no tsuki

To-night's Moon

Can there be anybody who
Won't write on to-night's moon?

Onitsura

The poet wonders if there can be any man of refinement who will not write a verse in praise of the bright harvest moon to-night.

[142]

あ の 山

あの山も けふのあつさの 行方哉

鬼 貫

Ano Yama

Ano yama mo
Kyō no atsusa no
Yukue kana

That Mountain

That mountain, too, is where
To-day's great heat has gone.

Onitsura

[143]

春　の　雨

狀見れば　江戸も降りけり　春の雨

鬼　貫

Haru no Ame

Jō mireba
Yedo mo furi-keri
Haru no ame

Spring Rain

Ah! I see from this letter that
The spring rain fell in Yedo, too.

Onitsura

A letter from a friend at Yedo tells that spring rain fell there too.

This seemingly meaningless verse mirrors well the sentiments of a Japanese poet, who considers spring rain one of the attractions of the season.

[144]

師弟のむすびせまほしくいはれし人に

花のない 木による人ぞ たゞならね

鬼　貫

Shitei no Musubi sema-hoshiku Iwareshi Hito ni

Hana no nai
Ki ni yoru hito zo
Tada nara-ne

To a Man who Asks me to be His Teacher

Ah! he is not a common man,
Who turns to a flowerless tree.

Onitsura

"A flowerless tree" means the poet himself.

A man who would take lessons from a poet of my little ability must be a man of wisdom.

Onitsura praises himself by praising his pupil-to-be.

[145]

水　鳥

水鳥の 重たく見えて 浮にけり

鬼　貫

Mizutori

Mizutori no
Omotaku miete
Ukini keri

The Waterfowl

The waterfowl looks heavy,
Yet lo! it floats on water.

Onitsura

[146]

蜘蛛の巣

蜘蛛の巣は あつきものなり 夏木立

鬼貫

Kumo no Su

Kumo no su wa
Atsuki mono nari
Natsu-kodachi

Cobwebs

How hot the cobwebs look,
Hanging on summer trees!

Onitsura

[**147**]

名　月

野も山も 晝かとぞ首の だるくこそ

鬼　貫

Meigetsu

No mo yama mo
Hiru ka tozo kubi no
Daruku koso

The Harvest Moon

The fields and hills looked clear as day;
I watched the moon till my neck ached.

Onitsura

蕉門の十哲

The Ten Great Disciples of Bashō

I

其　角（姓一寶井）

寶永四年歿　享年四十七

Kikaku (surname, Takarai)
A native of Yedo; a physician's son; a teacher of *haikai* by profession (1660–1707)

[148]

稲　妻

稲妻や　きのふは東　今日は西

其　角

Inazuma

Inazuma ya
Kinō wa higashi
Kyō wa nishi

Lightning

(A) **Yesterday it lightened east;**
Lo! to-day it lightened west.

(B) **The lightning was east yesterday;**
Lo! it was west to-day.

Kikaku

Some commentators interpret this verse as a simple realistic description, while others consider it to be a symbolic poem suggesting the transiency of life At any rate, it is an interesting *haiku.*

[149]

観心寺の牡丹

楠の　鎧ぬがれし　ぼたん哉

其　角

Kwanshin-ji no Botan

Kusunoki no
Yoroi nugareshi
Botan kana

The Peonies of the Kwanshin-ji Temple

Oh, beautiful peonies!—for love of which
Even Kusunoki took off his armour.

Kikaku

The Kwanshinji Temple, at Hino-o, in the province of Kawachi, has been famous for beautiful peonies from ancient times. It was the family temple of Kusunoki Masashige, who is celebrated for his unswerving loyalty to the Southern Court. After he committed *harakiri* at the Battle of Minatogawa, his head was buried in the precincts of the temple.

The verse means:—Even General Kusunoki, who was busy day and night, fighting for the cause of the Southern Court, removed his armour and enjoyed the sight of these peonies.

[150]

笠　の　雪

我雪と 思へば輕し 笠の上

其　角

Kasa no Yuki

Waga yuki to
Omoeba karushi
Kasa no ue

The Snow on My Hat

The snow upon my hat
Feels light, being mine own.

Kikaku

Snow is falling thickly and its silver flakes have accumulated on my hat. Since they are mine, they do not feel heavy but rather light and delightful.

This verse is very famous in connection with an *utazawa* or popular ditty which has adopted this verse, slightly altered, for its opening lines:—

Waga mono to omoeba karushi kasa no yuki

我が物と おもへば輕し 傘の雪

These lines, being exactly the same in meaning as the *haiku*, cannot be translated differently from the above rendering, except that *kasa* (傘) in the ditty means a large Japanese umbrella while *kasa* (笠) in the verse means a large hat like a cardinal's hat.

The subject of the *haiku* is not an actual experience but refers to a picture of Su Ton P'o (蘇東坡), a great Chinese man of letters, wearing a large snow-covered hat.

* * * * *

On my head-gear
Without plaint I bear
My snow load of care.

Trans. by Hidesaburō Saitō

[151]

初　雪

初雪や 内に居さうな 人は誰

其　角

Hatsuyuki

Hatsuyuki ya
Uchi ni isōna
Hito wa tare

The First Snow

'Tis the first snow! Who is likely
To stay indoors?

Kikaku

It is the first snowfall! I wonder if there can be anybody who stays indoors, quite indifferent to the charming sight. A commonplace verse.

* * * * *

'Tis the first snow,
Yet some one is indoors —
Who can it be?

Trans. by W. G. Aston

[152]

冬　の　蠅

憎まれて ながらふる人 冬の蠅

其　角

Fuyu no Hai

Nikumarete
Nagarōru hito
Fuyu no hai

Thc Winter Fly

He is a winter fly,
Who is hated and yet lives long.

Kikaku

A commonplace conceit.

[153]

花　の　雪

大佛 膝埋むらん 花の雪

其　角

Hana no Yuki

Ōbotoke
Hiza uzumu-ran
Hana no yuki

The Snow of Cherry-Flowers

Ah! the snow of cherry-flowers
Will bury the great Buddha's lap.

Kikaku

大佛 is pronounced *Daibutsu* in the present day but in ancient times it was often pronounced *Ōbotoke.*

Behold! in the spring breeze cherry-flowers, like snowflakes, are fluttering down all around. Their crystal petals will soon bury the lap of the great image of Buddha.

[154]

江 戸 の 春

鐘一つ 賣れぬ日はなし 江戸の春

其 角

Yedo no Haru

Kane hitotsu
Urenu hi wa nashi
Yedo no haru

Yedo in Spring

During the spring in great Yedo
Not a day passes but a temple bell is sold.

Kikaku

"A temple bell is sold" means that a new temple-bell is sold by a bell-maker.

During the springtime great Yedo is so prosperous in business that not a day passes on which at least one temple bell is not sold. Of course this is an exaggerated statement of the zenith of prosperity the Shōgun's capital enjoyed in those peaceful days. No mediocre poet would conceive of the sale of an expensive and gigantic temple bell as an instance of prosperity. A striking and clever idea typical of the talented Kikaku.

[155]

乞　食

乞食かな 天地を著たる 夏衣

其　角

Kojiki

Kojiki kana
Tenchi wo kitaru
Natsu-goromo

The Beggar

The blessed beggar! He has on
Heaven and earth for summer clothes.

Kikaku

It is a hot summer day. Behold the naked beggar! Having no house to live in, no family to care for, no property to be stolen, no worldly desires to torment him, he is sitting with a contented air in the shade of a great tree, with the blue sky for his canopy and the green grass for his robes. What a free, natural, simple and unrestrained life!

The striking, even subline, language, that gives the reader a delightful shock, striking him dumb, reveals to the full the poet's wonderful poetical powers and brilliant talent.

[156]

鶯 の 初 音

鶯の 身を逆さまに 初音かな

其 角

Uguisu no Hatsune

Uguisu no
Mi wo sakasama ni
Hatsune kana

The Nightingale's First Song

Head down, the nightingale
Is singing its first song.

Kikaku

A nightingale perched on a plum branch, with its head downward, is sweetly singing the first song since its arrival in the spring.

A simple realistic description of the sweet songster in an uncommon posture.

[157]

初　雪

初雪は 盆にもるべき ながめ哉

其　角

Hatsu-yuki

Hatsu-yuki wa
Bon ni moru beki
Nagame kana

The First Snow

The first snow is so beautiful,
I'd heap a tray with some of it.

Kikaku

[158]

冬の案山子

冬來ては 案山子にとまる 烏哉

其　角

Fuyu no Kagashi

Fuyu kite wa
Kagashi ni tomaru
Karasu kana

The Winter Scarecrow

The winter having come,
On scarecrows perch the crows.

Kikaku

The autumn harvest is over and winter has come. The scarecrows left unremoved in the cropped rice-fields stand in a sorry plight and have no duty to do; and some crows are perched on them.

A realistic sketch of a dreary scene in winter.

[159]

蛼　泣　く

猫に食はれしを　蛼の妻は　すだくらん

其　角

Kōrogi Naku

Neko ni kuwareshi wo
Kōrogi no tsuma wa
Sudaku ran

The Cricket Wails

Perchance the cricket is bemoaning
Her husband eaten by a cat.

Kikaku

This verse consists of twenty-one syllables—a redundancy seldom found in ancient *haiku*—but its rhythm is smooth.

A touching fantasy.

[160]

鳴　子　引

阿呆とは 鹿も見るらん 鳴子引

其　角

Naruko-Hiki

Ahō to wa
Shika mo miru ran
Naruko-hiki

The Bird-Clapper Man

Even deer may deem him a fool—
The puller of a bird-clapper.

Kikaku

A peasant who pulls a bird-clapper, a kind of scarecrow, to frighten birds away, may seem a fool even to deer.

A humorous fantasy.

[161]

踊

一長屋 錠をおろして 踊哉

其　角

Odori

Hito-nagaya
Jō wo oroshi te
Odori kana

The Dance

The folk of a tenement-house
Locked up their rooms and joined in a dance.

Kikaku

Open-air dances are held mainly by country people on the nights of July 13, 14, and 15—the Buddhist All Souls' Days—for the consolation of the dead. These dances are called "*Bon* dances."

All the members of the families who live in a tenement-house go away from their rooms and join in a *Bon* dance.

An interesting verse depicting the care-free, easy-going life of lower-class people.

[**162**]

名　月

名月や 疊の上に 松の影

其　角

Meigetsu

Meigetsu ya
Tatami no ue ni
Matsu no kage

The Bright Moon

What a beautiful moon! It casts
The shadow of pine boughs upon the mats.

Kikaku

The harvest moon is shining brightly. Behold! on the white mats of the poet's room is cast the shadow of the fantastic boughs of a pine tree growing in the garden.

One of the best known *haiku* of Kikaku.

[163]

郭　公

夢にくる 母をかへすか 郭公

其　角

Hototogisu

Yume ni kuru
Haha wo kaesu ka
Hototogisu

The Night Cuckoo

Oh, cuckoo, did you cry to drive away
My mother who was coming in my dream?

Kikaku

Kikaku's mother died when he was twenty-seven years old, and he often dreamed of her. One dawn, as usual, he was dreaming a delightful dream of her when a cuckoo's shrill cries suddenly broke his dream to his great disappointment.

[**164**]

蟬

隣から 此木憎むや 蟬の聲

其　角

Semi

Tonari kara
Kono ki nikumu ya
Semi no koe

Cicadas

Perchance my neighbours hate this tree,
On which cicadas cry aloud.

Kikaku

Probably there was a great tree in Kikaku's garden, and cicadas perched on it and cried loudly, which seemed to add to the intensity of the summer heat. In consequence perhaps his neighbours hated the tree.

A commonplace verse.

[**165**]

悼　工　齋

其人の 鼾さへなし 秋の蟬

其　角

Kōsai wo Itamu

Sono hito no
Ibiki sae nashi
Aki no semi

An Elegy on Kōsai

The autumn cicadas cry loud;
But ah! we can not hear even his snores.

Kikaku

Kōsai was a pupil of Bashō and a friend of Kikaku. A spontaneous exclamation of the grief-stricken poet.

[166]

舟 中 よ り

無い山の 富士に並ぶや 秋の暮

其 角

Shūchū Yori

Nai yama no
Fuji ni narabu ya
Aki no kure

From Aboard a Boat

Lo! mountains all unseen before come into sight
Beside Fuji, this autumn eve.

Kikaku

This is a distant view of Mount Fuji from a boat off Shinagawa, in the immediate vicinity of Tōkyō.

One autumn evening when the atmosphere was perfectly clear, small mountains which were usually invisible entered the poet's field of vision beside Mount Fuji.

[167]

夕　だ　ち

夕だちや 家をめぐりて 啼く家鴨

其　角

Yūdachi

Yūdachi ya
Ie wo meguri-te
Naku ahiru

A Summer Shower

A summer shower having come,
The ducks run quacking round the house.

Kikaku

A summer shower has come on a sudden. Dozens of ducks which played about the house were startled and ran round it quacking loudly. This realistic description of an actual scene is vivid enough to convey the quacking to the reader's mind's ear. All commentators unite in admiring the power of this verse.

[168]

雨　蛙

雨蛙 芭蕉にのりて 戰ぎけり

其　角

Ama-gaeru

Ama-gaeru
Bashō ni nori-te
Soyogi keri

A Tree-Frog

See how a tree-frog is swaying,
Perched on a banana leaf.

Kikaku

What a refreshing scene!—a tiny green frog swaying on a large graceful banana leaf waving in a fragrant breeze of early summer. Remember that all frogs are considered by Japanese poets to be sweet to listen to and beautiful to look at. They are a favourite subject of Japanese artists.

[169]

櫻

文は跡に 櫻さし出す 使かな

其 角

Sakura

Fumi wa ato ni
Sakura sashidasu
Tsukai kana

Cherry-Blossoms

The messenger, before giving the note,
Handed me branches of cherry-blossoms.

Kikaku

Two or three branches of beautiful cherry-blossoms, accompanied by a letter, were brought to the poet by a messenger from the Myōkyō-Bō, a Buddhist temple at Ueno. The quick-witted messenger, instead of handing him the note first, as would be done by an ordinary messenger, handed him the cherry-branches first and then the note.

"跡に" ought to have been written "後に."

A delightful verse—a typical example of artless art.

[170]

夕 涼 み

夕涼み よくぞ男に 生れける

其 角

Yūsuzumi

Yūsuzumi
Yokuzo otoko ni
Umare keru

Enjoying the Evening Cool

I am enjoying th' evening cool.
How lucky I was born a man!

Kikaku

In order to realize the full significance of this verse it is necessary to know that in Japan from olden times men have been allowed much greater freedom in the matter of garments and etiquette than has been permitted to women. When enjoying the evening cool in summer, common men often sit down on the mat cross-legged and half naked, sometimes entirely naked, while women, properly dressed, sit down respectfully. The poet congratulates himself on his good luck in having been born a man, who can enjoy the evening cool in a free and easy posture.

Taking the cool at eve, I do
Rejoice that I was born a man.

Trans. by Basil Hall Chamberlain

[171]

三　日　月

蜻蛉や 狂ひしづまる 三日の月

其　角

Mikazuki

Tombō ya
Kurui-shizumaru
Mika no tsuki

A Quarter Moon

On the rise of a crescent moon,
The dragonflies ceased their mad flight.

Kikaku

蜻蛉 is generally pronounced *tombo* but somethims *tombō*.

The countless dragonflies which were madly darting about in the setting sun have stopped their flight and disappeared somewhere on the rise of a slender crescent.

[172]

蚤　の　跡

きられたる 夢はまことか 蚤の跡

其　角

Nomi no Ato

Kirare-taru
Yume wa makoto ka
Nomi no ato

A Flea-Bite

Was the dream real, that I was cut down?
Nay, but I saw a flea-bite on me.

Kikaku

* * * * *

Is my dream true? Am I cut down?
Or was I bitten by a flea?

Trans. by Basil Hall Chamberlain

The Ten Great Disciples of Bashō

II

嵐 雪 (姓一服部)

寶永四年歿 享年五十四

Ransetsu (surname, Hattori) A samurai of lower rank; later a Buddhist priest: a native of Enami in Awaji Province (1653–1707)

[**173**]

元 日

元日や 晴れて雀の 物がたり

嵐 雪

Gwanjitsu

Gwanjitsu ya
Harete suzume no
Monogatari

New Year's Day

The sky has cleared on New Year's Day,
And sparrows chatter merrily.

Ransetsu

On New Year's Day, the happiest and most sacred day, the weather has proved to be exceptionally beautiful. All the people feel joyful, of course, and even little birds seem fo share their joy. The sparrows twitter so lustily that, it seems as if a merry conversation is going on among them.

Quite a beautiful verse with an exceedingly smooth rhythm—appropriate to the occasion.

[174]

早　春

梅一輪　一輪ほどの　暖さ

嵐　雪

Sōshun

Ume ichirin
Ichirin hodo no
Atataka-sa

Early Spring

The warmth grows by degrees;
One plum-blossom after another blooms.

Ransetsu

The mild warmth of early spring is increasing little by little as the lingering cold of winter recedes. An unmistakable sign of the waxing warmth—the plum-blossoms, the pioneers of spring flowers, are blooming one after another day by day.

The verse is commonplace in content but its beautiful rhetoric and smooth rhythm have made it very famous.

[175]

露 の 玉

草の葉を 遊びありけよ 露の玉

嵐 雪

Tsuyu no Tama

Kusa no ha wo
Asobi-arike yo
Tsuyu no tama

Beads of Dew

Beads of dew, play about
From one grass leaf to another.

Ransetsu

[176]

霞

武藏野の 幅にはせばき 霞哉

嵐 雪

Kasumi

Musashino no
Haba niwa sebaki
Kasumi kana

The Haze

The haze is too narrow
To fill the Musashino Plain.

Ransetsu

The Musashino Plain was in ancient times so wide a tract of land that, as poets sing, even the moon rose from and set among its grasses.

Now a picturesque spring haze is floating over the extensive plain with few hamlets, but it is not wide enough to fill the entire area of the field.

The purpose of the verse is to emphasize the size of the plain. The verse does not seem to have a high value.

[177]

け ふ の 月

海も山も 坊主にしたり けふの月

嵐 雪

Kyō no Tsuki

Umi mo yama mo
Bōzu ni shitari
Kyō no tsuki

The Moon of To-night

The moon of this night makes
All fields and mountains bald.

Ransetsu

The harvest moon bathes the fields and mountains in such a flood of bright beams that they all look quite naked.

[178]

天　の　川

眞夜中や　ふりかはりたる　天の川

嵐　雪

Ama-no-gawa

Mayonaka ya
Furikawari taru
Ama-no-gawa

The Heaven's River

(The Milky Way)

'Tis dead of night. Behold the Milky Way;
Its situation is entirely changed.

Ransetsu

Gazing up at the firmament at midnight, the poet is surprised to find the Milky Way in a situation entirely different from that in which he saw it earlier.

A manifestation of the poet's pious wonderment toward a solemn mystery of the heavens.

[179]

加茂河原の夕涼み

來る水の 行く水洗ふ 涼み哉

嵐 雪

Kamo-gawara no Yūsuzumi

Kuru-mizu no
Yuku-mizu arō
Suzumi kana

Cooling in the Kamo River-Bed

I enjoy the cool. The coming water
Washes the departing water.

Ransetsu

This was composed extempore when the poet cooled himself at the bed of the Kamo River, which flows through the east of Kyōto. Below the bench the crystal water is rippling slowly and softly over the bed of pebbles. The coming water flows after the departing water as if washing it. The beholder is filled with a refreshing feeling.

A beautiful verse with a delightful rhythm.

[180]

名 月

青空に 松をかいたり 今日の月

嵐 雪

Meigetsu

Aozora ni
Matsu wo kaitari
Kyō no tsuki

The Harvest Moon

At dusk the harvest moon
Paints a pine-tree against the blue.

Ransetsu

On the top of the eastern mountain, a gigantic pine-tree looms in bold relief against the blue sky at dusk. The harvest moon peering above the mountain intensifies the eerie silhouette of the pine. A picturesque scene. The bold statement, "*Paints* a pine tree," is unique.

[181]

黄菊と白菊

黄菊白菊　其ほかの名は　なくもがな

嵐　雪

Kigiku to Shiragiku

Kigiku shiragiku
Sono hoka no nawa
Nakumo gana

Yellow and White Chrysanthemums

Yellow and white chrysanthemums;
Would that there were no other names!

Ransetsu

There are many kinds of chrysanthemum, and not a few of them are beautiful, of course; but the poet is quite content with two kinds, the yellow and the white; indeed, he rather wishes there were no other names, namely no other chrysanthemums.

I have spoken rather disparagingly of this verse in the chapter, "*Haiku* and Epigrams"; but it is generally considered a masterpiece. Even Kikaku is said to have praised it highly. At any rate, it is representative of Ransetsu.

* * * * *

Chrysanthèmes jaunes, chrysanthèmes blancs:
Ah! que je voudrais qu'il n'y eût
D'autres noms que ceux-là!

Traduit par Michel Revon

[182]

名　月

名月や　烟這ゆく　水の上

嵐　雪

Meigetsu

Meigetsu ya
Keburi hai-yuku
Mizu no ue

The Harvest Moon

How brightly the harvest moon shines!
Vapour creeps upon the water.

Ransetsu

The poet is comtemplating the harvest moon at a lake or a great river. In the brilliant moonbeams mist floats upon the water and moves slowly as if crawling. From autumn to early winter vapour often rises from lakes and rivers.

An excellent realistic description.

Keburi or *kemuri* (烟) generally means "smoke" and sometimes "vapour," as is exemplified by the following *tanka* in the ***Fuboku Shū*** (夫木集):—

朝日さす 雪げのけぶり 打ち靡き
吉野の山も 見えず霞める

Asahi sasu *Yuki-ge no keburi* *Uchinabiki*
Yoshino-no-yama mo *Miezu kasumeru*

The vapour curling from the snow
Thawing in the bright morning sun
Is wafted to Mount Yoshino
Till it is quite veiled in the haze.

[**183**]

飢えたる胡蝶

繪の菊に けさは餓えたる 胡蝶かな

嵐 雪

Uetaru Kochō

E no kiku ni
Kesa wa ue taru
Kochō kana

A Hungry Butterfly

This morn a hungry butterfly
Tries to light on painted chrysanthemums.

Ransetsu

This seems to be a pure fantasy. It is doubtful whether a painting would attract a butterfly, which is possessed of a sharp sense of smell.

[184]

東　山

蒲團著て 寢たる姿や 東山

嵐　雪

Higashi-Yama

Futon kite
Netaru sugata ya
Higashi-yama

Mount Higashi

Lo! Mount Higashi looks
Like a man lying under quilts.

Ransetsu

Higashi-yama is a beautiful, low, flat mountain situated to the east of Kyōto.

This rather humorous verse is very famous and generally praised in that it exactly describes the appearance of the mountain.

[185]

薄

嵯峨中の 淋しさくゝる 薄かな

嵐 雪

Susuki

Saga jū no
Sabishi-sa kukuru
Susuki kana

The Pampas Grass

The pampas grass sums up
The lonesomeness of all Saga.

Ransetsu

Saga is a beautiful village situated to the west of Kyōto, as above stated. In the poet's day it was a lonely place sprinkled with Buddhist temples, and pampas grass seems to have abounded there. The pampas grass waving in the autumn wind excites a feeling of melancholy loneliness.

A beautiful verse.

[186]

蟬

あな悲し 鳶にとらるゝ 蟬の聲

嵐 雪

Semi

Ana kanashi
Tobi ni tora-ruru
Semi no koe

A Cicada

How heart-rendering the cry of
A cicada caught by a hawk!

Ransetsu

Who can resist the pathos of this tiny verse?

[187]

歸　雁

順禮に　打まじり行く　歸雁かな

嵐　雪

Kigan

Junrei ni
Uchi-majiri yuku
Kigan kana

Wild Geese Flying Home

Lo! mingled with the pilgrims,
The wild geese are flying home.

Ransetsu

A picture of two simultaneous processions—a band of Buddhist pilgrims wending their way, chanting hymns, and above them a flock of wild geese flying back northward, crying lonesomely. "Mingled with" is of course a figure of speech.

A picturesque scene in mid-spring.

[188]

辭　世

一葉散る 咄一葉散る 風のうへ

嵐　雪

Jisei

Hitoha chiru
Totsu hitoha chiru
Kaze no ue

The Death Verse

One leaf flutters down in the wind;
Another leaf drifts down, alas!

Ransetsu

The chilly autumn wind is blowing. Now one leaf flutters down, now another leaf flutters down. Alas! one after another, all the leaves fall down in the wind. This is the common lot of all men.

"The boast of heraldry, the pomp of power,
And all the beauty, all that wealth e'er gave,
Await alike the inevitable hour;
The paths of glory lead but to the grave."

* * * * *

A leaf whirls down, alackaday!
A leaf whirls down upon the breeze.

Trans. by Basil Hall Chamberlain

A single leaf, in fluttering way—
Alas! a single leaf, in fluttering way,
Floats down the wind to-day.

Trans. by Curtis Hidden Page

The Ten Great Disciples of Bashō

III

丈　草（姓一內藤）
寳永元年歿　享年四十三
Jōsō (surname, Naitō)
Born a samurai of Inuyama Clan, Owari Province; later a Buddhist priest (1661–1704)

[**189**]

冬　の　月

雪よりは　寒し白髮に　冬の月

丈　草

Fuyu no Tsuki

Yuki yori wa
Samushi shiraga ni
Fuyu no tsuki

The Winter Moon

Colder than snow it is indeed —
The winter moon on my grey hair!

Jōsō

[190]

梟

辻堂に 梟たてこむ 月夜かな

丈　草

Fukuro

Tsujidō ni
Fukuro tatekomu
Tsukiyo kana

An Owl

What a bright moonlit night! An owl
Took refuge in the wayside shrine.

Jōsō

The harvest moon shone so brightly that an owl which had gone astray out of a near-by wood flew into the wayside shrine for shade.

A *tsuji-dō* is a small wayside edifice dedicated to Buddha for the protection of travellers.

[191]

小　鴨

水底を 見て來た顔の 小鴨かな

丈　草

Kogamo

Mina-zoko wo
Mite kita kao no
Kogamo kana

The Teal

The teal wears such a look as if
It had gazed into the water's depths.

Jōsō

The teal—a small handsome duck—which dived into the water, has come again to the surface with a triumphant look as if it is saying, "Ah! I have been observing the bottom of the water. It was a beautiful sight."

* * * * *

The teal, with face fresh from the sight
Of what below the water lies.

Trans. by Basil Hall Chamberlain

[192]

銀 世 界

野も山も 雪に取られて なにもなし

丈 草

Ginsekai

No mo yama mo
Yuki ni torarete
Nani mo nashi

A Silvery World

The snow has taken all the fields
And hills, and nothing has been left.

Jōsō

As far as eye can reach, the world is covered with a vast silvery sheet. Hill and dale, tree and field, all alike clothed in virgin white. The figure, " The snow has taken " is interesting.

* * * * *

Nothing remaineth ; for the snow
Hath blotted out both moor and hill.

Trans. by Basil Hall Chamberlain

[193]

啄 木 鳥

啄木鳥の 枯木さがすや 花の中

丈 草

Kitsutsuki

Kitsutsuki no
Kareki sagasu ya
Hana no naka

The Woodpecker

The woodpecker looks for dead trees
Among the cherry-trees in bloom.

Jōsō

What an unæsthetic bird!

* * * * *

What! mid the flowers the woodpecker
Is seeking out a withered tree.

Trans. by Basil Hall Chamberlain

[194]

雲　雀

朝ごとに 同じ雲雀か 屋根の空

丈　草

Hibari

Asa goto ni
Onaji hibari ka
Yane no sora

The Skylark

Perchance it is the same lark which sings sweetly,
Every morn in the sky above my roof.

Jōsō

[195]

木　の　葉

水底の 岩に落つく 木の葉かな

丈　草

Kono-ha

Mina-zoko no
Iwa ni ochi-tsuku
Konoha kana

The Leaves

The fallen leaves have sunk and settled
Upon a rock below the water.

Jōsō

* * * * *

Behold the leaf that sinks and clings
Below the water to a rock!

Trans. by Basil Hall Chamberlain

[196]

秋　の　蟬

ぬけがらと 並びて死ぬる 秋の蟬

丈　草

Aki no Semi

Nuke-gara to
Narabite shinuru
Aki no semi

An Autumn Cicada

An autumn cicada lies dead
Side by side with its shell cast off.

Jōsō

A melancholy sight.

* * * * *

In autumn a cicada dead
Beside the shell that it cast off.

Trans. by Basil Hall Chamberlain

Autumn. And a cricket's shell—
Beside it, the dead cricket. Well......
Life—and fate.

Trans. by Curtis Hidden Page

Une cigale de l'automne,
Morte à côté
De sa coque vide!

Traduit par Michel Revon

* * * * *

The Ten Great Disciples of Bashō

IV

去　來 (姓一向井)
寶永元年歿　享年五十三
Kyorai (surname, Mukai)
A native of Nagasaki; resided at Kyōto; a Confucianist's son; a master of *haikai* (1651-1704)

[**197**]

元　　日

元日や 家にゆづりの 太刀はかむ

去　來

Gwanjitsu

Gwanjitsu ya
Ie ni yuzuri no
Tachi hakan

New Year's Day

It is New Year's Day; I would wear
The sword, an heirloom of my house.

Kyorai

A natural impulse for the poet who was well versed in military arts as well as in literature.

[198]

雪　の　門

應々と　言へど叩くや　雪の門

去　來

Yuki no Kado

Ō-ō to
Iedo tataku ya
Yuki no kado

The Snow-Covered Gate

I answered, "Yes. Yes," but
The snow-covered gate was still knocked at.

Kyorai

門 is pronounced either *kado* or *mon.*

It was a night of heavy snowfall. Not a soul stirred out in the snow, and silence regined all round. Suddenly a faint knocking was heard at the closed gate. So the poet answered "Yes. Yes," but his answer seemed to be inaudible to the visitor, who still continued to knock at the snow-covered gate.

A beautiful verse.

[199]

名　月

名月や　海もおもはず　山も見ず

去　來

Meigetsu

Meigetsu ya
Umi mo omowazu
Yama mo mizu

The Bright Moon

What a bright moon! I neither think
Of the sea nor view the mountain.

Kyorai

The poet was too much absorbed in the contemplation of the moon to think of the sea or to view the mountain.

[200]

雪　の　朝

旅人の　外は通らず　雪の朝

去　來

Yuki no Asa

Tabibito no
Hoka wa tōrazu
Yuki no asa

A Snowy Morning

A snowy morning;
None but travellers pass.

Kyorai

[201]

念　佛

すずしさの 野山にみつる 念佛かな

去　來

Nebutsu

Suzushisa no
No yama ni mitsuru
Nebutsu kana

The Chanting of Buddhist Prayers

The chanting of the prayers fills
The field and mountain with cool air.

Kyorai

念佛 is pronounced in three ways:—*nebutsu, nenbutsu* and *nebuchi.*

On a summer day a large congregation gathered at a great Buddhist temple is chanting prayers loudly in chorus with the sound of a big *mokugyo* or wooden gong. The chanting is so musical and delightful that it seems to fill with cool air the field and mountain close by the temple.

A spontaneous utterance of the pious poet.

[202]

曾　我　兄　弟

兄弟が 顔見合はすや 時鳥

去　來

Kyōdai

Kyōdai ga
Kao miawasu ya
Hototogisu

The Brothers

At the shrill cry of a night cuckoo
The brothers looked at each other.

Kyorai

The brothers are the Soga Brothers celebrated for the revenge of their father's death.

It was late on a dark night during the Rainy Season that they stole into their mortal enemy's camp for the bloody deed. Just then a cuckoo cried a shrill tragic cry (the night-cuckoo's cry is often considered by poets to be extremely tragic) in the sky. Moved by sudden deep emotion, the brothers, who carried torches, exchanged significant glances.

A weird moment.

[**203**]

長　刀

何事ぞ 花見る人の 長刀

去　來

Naga-gatana

Nanigoto zo
Hana miru hito no
Naga-gatana

A Long Sword

What! A flower-gazer
Carrying a long sword!

Kyorai

What an unæsthetic man who wears a long sword among the gay people quite given up to the contemplation of the beautiful cherry-blossoms!

* * * * *

A sabre! what has such to do
On one who comes to view the flowers?

Trans. by Basil Hall Chamberlain

Le long sabre
D'un homme qui regarde les fleurs,
Oh! qu'est-ce que cela?

Traduit par Michel Revon

[204]

土 用 干

鎧著て つかれためさん 土用干

去 來

Doyō-Boshi

Yoroi kite
Tsukare tamesan
Doyō-boshi

Summer Airing of Clothes

The summer airing of clothes—I will put on
The armour to see how soon I shall get tired.

Kyorai

Doyō-boshi is airing clothes and other things in midsummer.

Now that the armour, as well as the clothes, has been taken out from its chest for airing, the poet would wear it to see how effeminate he has become in consequence of the piping times of peace. A verse typical of the poet alive with martial ardour.

[205]

妹千子身まかりけるに

手の上に 悲しく消ゆる 螢かな

去 來

Imōto Chine Mimakari Keru Ni

Te no ue ni
Kanashiku kiyuru
Hotaru kana

On the Death of My Younger Sister Chine

Ah! the firefly has perished
Pitifully on my hand.

Kyorai

Quite appropriately the premature death of a lovely sister of delicate health is likened to a readily perishing firefly.

[206]

時 鳥 と 雲 雀

時鳥 鳴くや雲雀の 十文字

去 來

Hototogisu to Hibari

Hototogisu
Naku-ya hibari no
Jūmonji

The Cuckoo and the Skylark

The crying cuckoo draws a cross
Against the soaring lark.

Kyorai

The cuckoo flies in a straight, horizontal line while the skylark soars up in a perpendicular line. Therefore a flying cuckoo draws a cross against a soaring lark's course.

[207]

暑 さ

石も木も 眼に光る 暑さかな

去 來

Atsusa

Ishi mo ki mo
Manako ni hikaru
Atsusa kana

The Heat

What heat! Both stones and trees
Glare on the eye.

Kyorai

[208]

農　　夫

動くとも 見えで畑打つ 男かな

去　來

Nōfu

Ugoku to mo
miede hata utsu
Otoko kana

The Peasant

Lo! the peasant seems not to stir,
Yet he is tilling the field hard.

Kyorai

A tranquil field scene on a sweet spring day.

[209]

眞　帆　片　帆

いそがしや 沖の時雨の 眞帆片帆

去　來

Maho Kataho

Isogashi ya
Oki no shigure no
Maho kataho

Full Sails and Reefed Sails

How busy the full sails and the reefed
At sea in the winter shower!

Kyorai

A picturesque description of silvery sails plying busily in a winter shower.

* * * * *

What haste! a shower in the offing,
And sails set straight, and sails set aslant.

Trans. by Basil Hall Chamberlain

[210]

雲 の 峰

夕暮や 禿げ並びたる 雲の峰

去 來

Kumo no Mine

Yūgure ya
Hage-narabi taru
Kumo no mine

Peaks of Clouds

'Tis evening; what a row of
Bare peaks of summer clouds!

Kyorai

[211]

月　見

月見せん　伏見の里の　捨廓

去　來

Tsukimi

Tsukimi sen
Fushimi no sato no
Sute-guruwa

The Moon-Viewing

I will go to gaze at the moon
From the deserted castle-courts of Fushimi.

Kyorai

Fushimi Castle situated on the hill of Momoyama on the Yodogawa near Kyōto was the palace of the Taikō Hideyoshi (1536–1598), the Napoleon of Japan. It was the grandest edifice ever built in Japan, but it was given over to flames soon after the demise of the warrior-statesman.

The smooth and quiet rhythm of this verse perfectly harmonizes with the poet's love of historical associations.

The Ten Great Disciples of Bashō

V

許　六 (姓一森川)
正徳五年歿　享年六十
Kyoroku (surname, Morikawa)
A samurai of Hikone Clan
(1655–1715)

[212]

土　用　干

一竿は　死装束や　土用干
許　六

Doyō-Boshi

Hito-sawo wa
Shini-shōzoku ya
Doyō-boshi

Summer Airing of Garments

Summer airing of clothes —
On one pole hang death-clothes.
Kyoroku

"Death-clothes" are clothes which old people prepare while alive for their grave-clothes. They are often made of a rich silk of pure white. This custom belongs to Old Japan.

It is a fine midsummer day. The whole family's garments, hanging pictures, books and so forth are hung on poles or strings for airing. On one pole are hung white death-clothes, while on the other poles are gay-coloured garments. A solemn contrast.

[213]

菜 の 花

菜の花の 中に城あり 郡山

許 六

Nanohana

Nanohana no
Naka ni shiro ari
Kōriyama

Rape-Flowers

At Kōriyama there is a castle
Amidst an expanse of rape-flowers.

Kyoroku

Kōriyama, a large town in the province of Yamato, was a prosperous castle-town in the feudal Japan.

A realistic verse presenting to the mind's eye a vivid picture of a white donjon and white walls glittering amidst an expanse of golden flowers waving in a spring breeze.

[214]

大 名 の 閨

大名の 閨にも寝たる 寒さかな

許 六

Daimio no Neya

Daimio no
Neya nimo netaru
Samusa kana

A Daimio's Bedroom

I've slept in a daimio's bedroom;
But ah! I felt cold even there.

Kyoroku

Nature is no respecter of persons.

[215]

秣

己がはむ 秣を {つけて / 負て} 夏野かな

許　六

Magusa

Ono ga hamu
Magusa wo {tsukete / oute}
Natsuno kana

Fodder

Lo! on the summer moor
A horse carries its own fodder.

Kyoroku

A refreshing sketch.

[216]

野　分

一番に 案山子をこかす 野分哉

許　六

Nowaki

Ichiban ni
Kagashi wo kokasu
Nowaki kana

An Autumn Tempest

The autumn tempest has blown down
The scarecrows first of all.

Kyoroku

Humour and pathos combined.

[217]

朝　顔

看經の 間を朝顔の 盛哉

許　六

Asagao

Kankin no
Ma wo asagao no
Sakari kana

Morning-Glories

Ah! the morning-glories are at their best
While I am chanting my morning prayers.

Kyoroku

Alas! how speedily the charming flowers fade!

[218]

行　水

行水の 背中をてらす 夏の月

許　六

Gyōzui

Gyōzui no
Senaka wo terasu
Natsu no tsuki

An Open Air Bath

Taking an open air hot bath,
The summer moon shines on my back.

Kyoroku

A summer evening's joy given to country people.

[219]

鴨　の　聲

明がたや 城をとりまく 鴨の聲

許　六

Kamo no Koe

Akegata ya
Shiro wo torimaku
Kamo no koe

The Quacking of Wild Ducks

It is dawn. The castle is surrounded
By the quacking of wild ducks.

Kyoroku

It is early dawn. The castle is wrapt in haze and slumber; but in the moat around it wild ducks are calling noisily. Their cries seem to surround the castle, as if it were surrounded by the war-cries of a hostile army.

A powerful verse.

[220]

雲　雀

白雲の 上に聲ある 雲雀かな

許　六

Hibari

Shira-kumo no
Ue ni koe aru
Hibari kana

Skylarks

There are voices above white clouds —
They are the skylarks' notes.

Kyoroku

The Ten Great Disciples of Bashō

VI

杉　風（姓一杉山）
享保十七年歿　享年八十六
Sampū (surname, Sugiyama)
A native of Yedo; a rich fish purveyor to the Shogun's household (1646–1732)

[221]

名　な　き　草

名は知らず　草毎に花　あはれなり

杉　風

Nanaki Kusa

Nawa shirazu
Kusa goto ni hana
Aware nari

Nameless Herbs

Their names are unknown, but these herbs —
All of them have lovely flowers.

Sampū

Aware generally means "pitiable" but sometimes "lovely."

In the autumn plain thousands of herbs whose names are unknown have burst forth into lovely flowers.

A simple naturalistic description fitting for lovely but quiet autumn flowers.

[222]

夕　立

撫子を　打つ夕立や　さもあらき
杉　風

Yūdachi

Nadeshiko wo
Utsu yūdachi ya
Samo araki

A Summer Shower

How hard the shower falls
Upon the lovely pinks!

Sampū

Yūdachi is a summer shower but "the shower" will do in a translation of this verse which contains another "season word," "pinks."

Showing deep sympathy for tiny flowers.

[223]

雲　雀

子や待ん　あまり雲雀の　高あがり
杉　風

Hibari

Ko ya matan
Amari hibari no
Taka-agari

The Skylark

The skylarks are soaring too high;
Surely their young ones wait for them.

Sampū

* * * * *

Oh! how its young ones must be waiting—
For all too high ascends the lark!

Trans. by Basil Hall Chamberlain

Comme vont attendre ses enfants,
Pendant que s'élève si haut,
A l'excès, l'alouette!

Traduit par Michel Revon

[**224**]

冬　の　月

襟巻に　首引入れて　冬の月

杉　風

Fuyu no Tsuki

Erimaki ni
Kubi hiki-ire te
Fuyu no tsuki

The Winter Moon

With my neck in a comforter,
I viewed the winter moon.

Sampū

Moonlight in winter, and I draw
My neck within my comforter.

Trans. by Basil Hall Chamberlain

[225]

雪　見

覺悟して 風引きに行く 雪見かな

杉　風

Yukimi

Kakugo shite
Kaze hiki ni yuku
Yukimi kana

Snow-Viewing

Well, I'll go and see the snow scene,
Prepared for risk of taking cold.

Sampū

On this occasion the poet had a slight indisposition, and yet he went out to view the snow scene, at the risk of taking cold.

[226]

五　月　雨

五月雨に 蛙の泳ぐ 戸口かな

杉　風

Samidare

Samidare ni
Kawazu no oyogu
Toguchi kana

The May Rains

Lo! frogs are swimming at the door
In May rains' overflow.

Sampū

The May rains having continued for several days, the water has overflowed up to the front door of the poet's house, and some frogs are swimming in the pool at the door. In order to appreciate this verse it is necessary, as stated above, to remember that Japanese poets consider the frog a lovely creature with a sweet voice.

[227]

啞　蟬

啞蟬の　啼かぬ梢も　あはれなり

杉　風

Oshi-Zemi

Oshi-zemi no
Nakanu kozue mo
Aware nari

Dumb Cicadas

The bough, too, is a sorry sight
To which the dumb cicadas cling.

Sampū

The noisy cicada is one of the summer nuisances, but a dumb cicada is pitiable; and so the bough to which dumb cicadas cling is a sorry sight.

This sentiment is typical of a compassionate poet.

[228]

雪　と　雨

けさは雪　雨になりしか　春のとが

杉　風

Yuki to Ame

Kesa wa yuki
Ame ni narishi-ka
Haru no toga

Snow and Rain

Has the snow turned to rain this morning?
Spring is to blame for it.

Sampū

The beautiful snow which has been falling since yesterday has changed into rain this morning, to the disappointment of the poet; and this change is due to the Spring which is growing milder day by day.

The Ten Great Disciples of Bashō

VII

支　考（姓—各務）

享保十六年歿　享年六十七

Shikō (surname, Kagami)
A native of Kitano in Mino Province; first a Buddhist priest, later a physician (1664–1731)

[229]

紅　　葉

うらやまし　美しう成て　散る紅葉

支　考

Momiji

Urayamashi
Utsukushū natte
Chiru momiji

The Maple Leaves

How I envy maple leafage
Which turns beautiful and then falls!

Shikō

The *yamazakura* or wild cherry, which scatters its flowers soon after they attain the zenith of their beauty, is considered a symbol of the spirit of the samurai who would prefer death to disgrace and faces death with heroism.

Again we have the saying "Better be a jewel broken into pieces than a tile kept whole." These traditional ideas led the writer of this verse to admire the maple leaves which turn beautiful and then are scattered like the wild cherry.

Another reading of this verse runs as follows:—

花よりも 美しくなりて ちる紅葉

Hana yori mo
Utsukushiku narite
Chiru momiji

The maple leafage turns more beautiful
Than cherry-flowers, then falls readily.

[230]

紅　葉

飛ぶ鳥の 羽もこがるゝ 紅葉かな

支　考

Momiji

Tobu tori no
Hàne mo kogaruru
Momiji kana

The Red Foliage

The red maple leaves shine so bright,
The wings of flying birds are scorched.

Shikō

An exaggeration, out of place.

[231]

峰　の　松

そこもとは 涼しさうなり 峰の松

支　考

Mine no Matsu

Sokomoto wa
Suzushi sō nari
Mine no matsu

The Pine-Tree on the Peak

Oh, how cool thou lookest!
Thou pine tree on the peak.

Shikō

[232]

あ　ら　し

鶯の 調子かえたる あらしかな

支　考

Arashi

Uguisu no
Chōshi kae taru
Arashi kana

A Tempest

What a violent tempest!
The nightingales have changed their tones.

Shikō

[233]

桃の花

船頭の 耳の遠さよ 桃の花

支考

Momo no Hana

Sendō no
Mimi no tōsa yo
Momo no hana

The Peach-Blossom

The peach-blossoms are beautiful;
But ah! the ferryman is deaf.

Shikō

Peach-blossoms blaze beautifully on both banks of the river. The poet would talk to the ferryman about them; but alas! he is deaf and plies his pole stolidly.

The Ten Great Disciples of Bashō

VIII

野坡 (姓一志多)
元文五年歿 享年七十八

Yaha (surname, Shida)
A native of Fukui in Echigo Province; first a merchant, later a master of *haikai* (1662–1740)

[234]

御　　慶

長松が 親の名で來る 御慶かな

野　坡

Gyokei

Chōmatsu ga
Oya no na de kuru
Gyokei kana

The New Year's Greetings

Chōmatsu comes in his father's name
To offer the New Year's greetings.

Yaha

During the first week of the New Year, particularly on New Year's Day, the Japanese call on their relatives and friends in their neighbourhood to offer the New Year's greetings. "Chōmatsu" is a humorous appellation often applied in Old Japan to a little boy, regardless of his real name. It is nearly equivalent to "Johnny."

It is a New Year's Day. Chōmatsu, somebody's little boy, in ceremonial clothes, assuming an important air, calls to offer congratulations, in the name of his father.

The interest of this verse consists in the humorous effect produced by a mixture of the comical name, the self-importance of the little fellow and the solemn occasion.

[235]

猫　の　戀

猫の戀 初手からないて 哀れ也

野　坡

Neko no Koi

Neko no koi
Shote kara naite
Aware nari

The Cat in Love

The cat in love is pitiable,
Caterwauling from the beginning.

Yaha

* * * * *

A cat's amours:—from the beginning
He caterwauls! he is to be pitied.

Trans. by Basil Hall Chamberlain

[236]

鶯

鶯や 門はまたまた 豆腐賣

野　坡

Uguisu

Uguisu ya
Kado wa tama-tama
Tōfu-uri

The Nightingale

The nightingale was singing sweet. Just then
A bean-curd vendor's noisy street-cry at the gate.

Yaha

A humorous contrast between sweet notes and a harsh cry.

* * * * *

The nightingale and, at the gate,
The unexpected bean-curd vendor.

Trans. by Basil Hall Chamberlain

Oh! le rossignol!
A la porte, juste à ce moment,
Le vendeur de tôfou!

Traduit par Michel Revon

[237]

菫

法度場の　垣より内は　菫かな

野　坡

Sumire

Hottoba no
Kaki yori uchi wa
Sumire kana

Violets

Behold! violets bloom within
The fence of the forbidden ground.

Yaha

The forbidden ground is enclosed with a fence, and inside the fence violets are in bloom all over the ground. The contrast between a disagreeable place and lovely tiny flowers constitutes an irony.

[238]

椿

はき掃除 してから椿 散りにけり

野 坡

Tsubaki

Haki-sōji
Shite kara tsubaki
Chiri ni keri

The Camellias

When I'd swept the garden thoroughly
Some camellia flowers dropped down.

Yaha

The poet is rather delighted to find that the ground is beautifully strewn with the handsome red and white petals.

* * * * *

After I've swept and tidied up,
Adown fall some camellias.

Trans. by Basil Hall Chamberlain

The Ten Great Disciples of Bashō

IX

北　枝（姓一立花）
金澤の人　享保三年歿
Hokushi (surname, Tachibana)
A native of Kanazawa; a sword-burnisher (died 1718)

[239]

焼け出されて

焼けにけり　されども花は　ちりすまし

北　枝

Yakedasarete

Yake ni keri
Saredomo hana wa
Chiri sumashi

Burnt Out

I am burnt out, but luckily
The flowers have had their glory and are gone.

Hokushi

The cherry trees, as well as my house, are burnt down; but fortunately it is after the flowers have duly bloomed and scattered. I have enjoyed their sight to my heart's content, and so I have nothing at all to regret.

The poet's house, together with cherry-trees in its garden, was destroyed by a great fire. His relatives and friends flocked to present their condolences. He expressed his gratitude and then, with perfect composure, showed them this verse.

* * * * *

Burnt out of house and home,
"And Winter coming on, alas!" you say,
It matters not. My flowers have had their day.

Trans. by Curtis Hidden Page

(Ma maison) a brûlé:
Néanmoins, les fleurs
Sont tombées et passées.

Traduit par Michel Revon

When the poet was burnt out again, his friend Shikō wrote the following verse for his consolation.

焼けにけり されども櫻 さかぬうち

Yake ni keri
Saredomo sakura
Sakanu-uchi

You are burnt out, but luckily
Before the cherry-flowers bloom.

Notice the easy-going mood of nature poets.

[240]

四睡が武府に行をり

牡丹散て 心もおかず 別れけり

北 枝

Shisui ga Bufu ni Yuku Ori

Botan chitte
Kokoro mo okazu
Wakare keri

To Shisui Departing for Yedo

The peony flowers having fallen,
We have parted without regrets.

Hokushi

The two poets, lovers of the peonies, parted without any regret because the beautiful flowers had already scattered.

[241]

雪 の 暮

傘の いくつ過行く 雪のくれ

北 枝

Yuki no Kure

Karakasa no
Ikutsu sugiyuku
Yuki no kure

A Snowy Evening

'Twas a snowy evening.
How many umbrellas went by?

Hokushi

Karakasa (傘) means the truly Japanese rain-umbrellas made of strong oiled paper and bamboo. These are coloured terra-cotta, blue, green, mauve and other beautiful tints, generally plain, with broad circular stripes of a different colour. The tinted light passing through the umbrella, reflected on its bearer, is a pleasure to an artist's eye.

[**242**]

蛙

田を賣りて いとゞねられぬ 蛙かな

北 枝

Kawazu

Ta wo urite
Itodo nerarenu
Kawazu kana

The Frog

I have sold my paddy-fields and now
The singing frogs but keep me wakeful.

Hokushi

The sweet song of the frog usually lulled the poet to sleep; but now the singing frogs in the field he had sold kept him awake.

[**243**]

名 月

月を松に 懸けたり外し ても見たり

北 枝

Meigetsu

Tsuki wo matsu ni
Kake-tari hazushi
Temo mitari

The Bright Moon

Now the bright moon was hung on the pine,
And now it was slipped off from the tree.

Hokushi

After "hung" is understood "by myself." The poet watched the moon from different viewpoints so that now it appeared to be hanging on the pine-tree, now it appeared to be off the tree. Remember that the full moon on a fantastic pine-tree is a favourite subject for poets as well as for artists.

This verse may be more exactly translated as follows:—

Now I hung the moon on the pine,
Now took it off the tree.

The Ten Great Disciples of Bashō

X

越 人 (姓—越智)
元禄十五年歿
Etsujin (surname, Ochi)
A samurai of Kumamoto Clan; later
a dyer at Nagoya (died 1702)

[**244**]

鮎

聲あらば 鮎も泣くらん 鵜飼舟

越 人

Ayu

Koe araba
Ayu mo naku ran
Ukai-bune

The *Ayu*

Had they a voice, *ayu* would cry
At sight of the cormorant boat.*

Etsujin

The *ayu* is a kind of fresh-water trout which is highly valued as food. As stated above,* *ayu* are often caught by cormorants manipulated by fishers aboard a boat called *ukai-bune* or "cormorant fishing boat."

[245]

花 に 埋 れ て

花に埋れて　夢より直に　死なん哉

越　人

Hana ni Umore te

Hana ni umore te
Yume yori jiki ni
Shinan kana

---

* See "The Cormorant Fishing Boat" by Bashō (P. 151).

Buried in Flowers

I long to pass away, straight from sweet dreams,
Buried in the cherry-flowers.

Etsujin

Fallen cherry-flowers are heaped up thickly in the poet's garden. What a fascinating sight! He wishes to be buried under the charming petals, to dream a sweet dream and so go to death without awakening from it.

Written in loving admiration of the cherry-flowers. The first line consists of seven syllables instead of the regular five, but the verse is a rhythmical and beautiful piece worthy of an old hand.

[**246**]

白 髪

行年や 親に白髪を かくしけり

越 人

Shiraga

Yuku-toshi ya
Oya ni shiraga wo
Kakushi keri

Grey Hair

Alas! another year has gone;
I've hid my grey hair from my parents.

Etsujin

In order to prevent them from realizing that the poet is getting old. A natural sentiment on the part of a dutiful son.

[247]

けふの月

蟲の音で　さては夜也　けふの月

越　人

Kyō no Tsuki

Mushi no ne de
Satewa yoru nari
Kyō no tsuki

The Bright Moon

(A) By insects' songs alone I knew
'Twas night. How bright the moon!

(B) The insects' songs alone told me 'twas night.
So brilliantly the full moon shone!

Etsujin

[248]

初雪

初雪を　見てから顔を　洗ひけり

越　人

Hatsu-yuki

Hatsu-yuki wo
Mite kara kawo wo
Arai keri

The First Snow

I looked out over the first snow
And *then* I washed my face.

Etsujin

Before washing his face in the morning, the poet took a look out over the beautiful scene of the first snow. This is the surface meaning, but there may be a deeper suggestion of the purity of the snow, and consequent instinctive self-cleansing.

[**249**]

け し の 花

ちるときの 心安さよ けしの花

越　人

Keshi-no-Hana

Chiru toki no
Kokoro yasusa yo
Keshi-no-hana

The Poppy-Flower

With what calm readiness
The poppy-flowers fall!

Etsujin

The simple, half-subjective description seems to suggest something profound.